Using Your Values

to Raise Your Child to Be an Adult You Admire

Using Your Values

to Raise Your Child to Be an Adult You Admire

Harriet Heath, Ph.D.

Illustrated by Anna Dewdney

PARENTING PRESS, INC.

Seattle, Washington

Edited by Carolyn J. Threadgill
Designed by Magrit Baurecht Design
Cover illustrations by Mits Katayama
Interior illustrations by Anna Dewdney

Library of Congress Cataloging-in-Publication Data
Heath, Harriet.
    Using your values to raise your child to be an adult you admire /
Harriet Heath; illustrated by Anna Dewdney
        p.   cm.
    Includes bibliographical references and index.
    ISBN 1-884734-36-7 (pbk.). -- ISBN 1-884734-37-5 (lib. bdg.). --
ISBN 1-884734-49-9 (cloth)
    1. Parenting. 2. Parenting--Moral and ethical aspects. 3. Values.
I. Dewdney, Anna.   II. Title
HQ755.8.H434   2000
649'. 1--dc21   99-26641

Parenting Press, Inc.
P.O. Box 75267
Seattle, Washington 98125-0267

World Wide Web site: *http://www.ParentingPress.com*
Telephone 1-800-992-6657

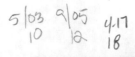

Contents

Acknowledgments

I want to thank the parents who told me, "It was the values that were so helpful. When we didn't know what to do we'd ask ourselves, 'What are our values here?'"

I want to thank my children who showed me how relevant values were to family life—a lesson I wish I'd learned while they were still young.

I want to thank my husband who proved through his research that values matter in the lives of effective people.

And I want to thank my editor, Carolyn Threadgill, and my publisher, Elizabeth Crary, for helping make a complex process understandable and useful for parents.

First Thoughts

Values . . . everybody is talking about nobody having any. Every time something horrible happens, people in the know tell us how our lack of values is responsible. They tell us specifically which values have disappeared from our culture. Our families are falling apart because parents have no values and are raising children who have none. Our country will self-destruct unless we get some soon, say the experts on all sides.

If you listen carefully, you will hear that every faction has different ideas of which values are the right ones to rescue us from imminent downfall. They each have different ideas about how people should behave even when they value the same thing.

So, what should we do? How should we reinstate values into our lives? The notions of what and how are often presented in shallow, trivial terms. To suggest that a few stories, some games, a night out serving meals to the homeless, or even weekly attendance at religious services are all it takes to instill values is to be naive about the process whereby people come to live according to certain values. Though those activities can be inspiring and motivational, they are not nearly enough.

My grandson (age 3) announced at the top of his voice, "That woman has a fat fanny!" as he and his mother stood in the grocery check-out line. He was being honest, reporting what he saw at eye level in front of him. If imparting values were so easy, his mother could have said, "Yes, my child, she has a fat fanny. I commend your honesty." But, if she values caring as well, how should she respond? The woman's feelings were undoubtedly hurt. How should my daughter teach her son about honesty and other values that might be important to her? Living by values and teaching them are more complicated than many would have us believe.

When my children were growing up, I slowly came to realize that values guided my parenting. The question was, which values was I using? Were they the ones I wanted my children to have? Now my daughters are mothers. We know which values are ours, and use them to guide our many discussions about how to handle situations with any one of my eight grandchildren.

As a parent educator, psychologist, researcher, and designer of life-changing programs at home and abroad, an integral part of my work has been to encourage parents to use their values as guides for their parenting and general family decisions. Over the past 30 years, parents have told me that our discussions about values gave them direction for their parenting. Again and again, they returned to their values for guidance.

I have found that all parents *do* have values. Some may have thought about them, but few have considered them when dealing with everyday situations. Even fewer parents have thought about how their values may affect their children 10 to 30 years down the road. For better or for worse, values—the principles upon which we base our behavior—guide us. The problem is that we are not used to thinking actively about our values, and we are therefore not accustomed to tapping into this potential source of parenting guidance.

THIS BOOK IS DIFFERENT

Identifying your values requires insightful thinking. You will find no superficial trivia here about how to save your family or the nation in one or a few brief acts. Instead, I will help you integrate your values into your family life and pass them on to your children. To do both of these things, you need to:

• know your values
• understand what they mean to you
• live your values
• model your values in ways your children can see and understand
• realize what a child must know and be able to do to live by a value
• understand the developmental steps a child must go through to live by a value
• recognize opportunities to teach values

Most authors and authorities apparently feel their personal values will be the very same ones held by all the parents they address. They seldom ask parents what *their* values are. However, I remember feeling angry and resentful when someone else told me what my values should be. I knew what kind of people I wanted my children to be and I resented some "expert" deciding that for me. I will not decide for you what your values should be. That is your business. One of my goals, however, is to help you *identify* what *your* values are.

Having said that, I do acknowledge at the outset drawing upon my own values in the examples I use to illustrate points and the process of integrating values into parenting. You are free to view my examples as *illustrations of the process,* not as declarations that these are the values you must hold.

You may question your right to require your child to live by the values you hold. Do not worry: when children become teenagers they will question your values as they search for those on which to base their lives. This natural and necessary stage of development is more difficult for children who have no firm foundation from which to start their explorations. It is your role as parent to provide such a foundation. Even if teenagers totally reject their parents' values (a rare outcome), they have a head start in figuring out what they value.

My other goal is to help you *nurture or teach* values. Values can be present at birth and then lost in a society that does not believe them worthwhile. For example, how do you preserve curiosity in a two-year-old who is constantly told, "Don't touch. Don't make a mess," or in a ten-year-old who hears repeatedly, "You ask too many questions."

Some values are complex, requiring inclination, knowledge, and skills to live by them. Caring is such a value. Finally, some values may conflict with one another. A mother called me not long ago because her daughter's guinea pig was dead. No food, no water in the cage. The daughter was terribly distraught. She knew she had neglected her pet. The mother's question was, "How do I handle this? I want my daughter to be responsible and I also want her to be emotionally healthy, not guilt-ridden for life." In this book, you and I will take up these challenges.

As you read *Using Your Values . . . ,* you will realize that everyday situations become opportunities to teach values. How you help your child enjoy the beach during summer vacation, for example, can be an opportunity to teach how to take care of the environment.

I wrote this book because I wish I had been more clearly aware of my values as guides when I was raising my children. I see my grandchildren being raised by parents who are aware of their values, and I wish this same confidence for you. Knowing your values makes nurturing children easier, giving direction to all those decisions you constantly are making. As the sailor has the stars and the traveler a map, you parents have your values to point the way.

1

Living with Values

Three-year-old Suzy rushed to greet her grandmother at the door. "Happy birthday," Grandma said, as the two gave each other big hugs.

Grandma handed Suzy a beautifully wrapped package. Suzy tore off the paper, opened the box, and found a soft, cuddly teddy bear inside. Her disappointment was clear as she threw down the teddy bear, her face contorted and red.

"I already have two," she said in a tight, squeaky voice and began to cry.

Parents pass on their values to their children by the way they handle each day's events, the seemingly insignificant ones as well as the potential crises. Suzy's parents will convey their values by how they respond to Suzy's behavior. Before we look in on what they may do, let us define the term *values.*

WHAT IS A VALUE?

Everyone has values. They are the principles on which people choose to base their behavior. Sometimes people are aware of their values and can state them; many people, however, have never stopped to consider exactly what values guide them. Different people have different values. Any two parents are likely to share some values and not others; sometimes their values may conflict. One may value material goods, the other prefer to have no more things than minimally necessary to survive. Some values, however, such as caring, responsibility, honesty, courage, loyalty, curiosity, and wisdom, are held by many people.

Also, cultures as a whole tend to emphasize some values over others. American culture, for example, values independence and individuality, while Japanese culture emphasizes cooperation and being part of the group; both value education.

How people show their values

People show their values through their *actions.* A person who believes in caring will check to see if an elderly neighbor needs anything or help a crying child who is lost in the mall. Someone who believes in being responsible will make sure to change the car's oil regularly, pay the bills on time, and keep an appointment. Yet another person who values clear thinking will consider carefully the pros and cons of traveling during a winter storm, or the outcome in the future of an action taken now.

How Suzy's parents respond to her disappointment will show their values. Their reaction can vary from saying and doing nothing to banishing Suzy to her room after giving her a spanking. What Suzy learns will depend on what they do.

If they value politeness and good manners, they might tell Suzy, "You can at least thank Grandma for remembering your birthday." They might also give her a time-out in her room to help her remember to be polite.

If they want Suzy to be in touch with her feelings, they would be more likely to acknowledge her disappointment: "You're disappointed that Grandma brought you a toy you already have."

If they want Suzy to be caring, they might help her to understand how her grandmother feels and to know what to say: "Grandma didn't know you already had that toy. She's feeling sad that you don't like her gift. Can you thank her for remembering your birthday?"

If Suzy's parents value all three principles of behavior—*politeness, caring,* and *being in touch with her feelings*—they might say, "We know you're disappointed that you already have a teddy bear. Grandma's feeling sad that you don't like her gift. Can you thank her anyhow and give her a hug?"

If Suzy's parents do not know what their values are, their response becomes unpredictable: one time Suzy is to be polite, another she is to be in touch with her feelings, and another her behavior is ignored and she is confused about how she is to act.

You can see that in any given situation various responses are possible. Which ones you choose will depend on how you view the situation—just a situation to be dealt with or an opportunity to teach your values, the principles of behavior you hold important.

TEACHING VALUES

Values are important to Derek and Bianca, parents of six-year-old Sean and four-year-old Jermaine. They had thought seriously about them when Sean was still a baby. What values did they want to instill in their son? What guides would he need to have a happy, fulfilling life? Their list of values included the ability to care, being aware of feelings, being competent, and having self-esteem. They had gathered information about their values to help them integrate these into their family life. Using their values to guide how they dealt with Sean and his little brother, Jermaine, had become quite routine, as a recent argument between the boys shows.

Derek was sorting the day's mail when he heard Sean scream at Jermaine.

"You can't do that! You're cheating! . . . I'm not gonna play with a cheater," Sean added disgustedly, as he jumped up and kicked the game board, sending pieces flying all over the floor.

Jermaine, looking surprised and hurt, started to cry.

To be able to care, a person must be able to learn about the situation. Derek models behavior based on the value as he asks the boys what happened and listens carefully to each boy's answer.

"Boys, what's the matter?"

"He moved his piece from here to here," replies Sean, pointing across the board.

"But I only wanted to be near Sean's piece," wails Jermaine. "Now he's ruined my game. The pieces are all lost!"

Reaching out to his younger son, Derek says, "Your game isn't ruined, Jermaine." Giving him a hug, he continues, "Let's find the pieces and put them back on the board."

Sniffling, the boys start collecting the pieces. Derek turns his attention to his older son.

"Remember what we talked about last night, Sean?" Derek says, speaking quietly and gently, with his hand on Sean's shoulder. "This is what we meant. Jermaine doesn't understand about rules yet like you do."

Valuing also that his boys be in touch with their feelings, Derek continues, "It's frustrating, isn't it, when both people don't understand a game in the same way? But kicking doesn't help. . . . We'd better count these

pieces to be sure we have them all. You can set the game up again."

To be able to care requires understanding another person's perspective. At six, Sean is beginning to be able to do this. His parents had already tried to help him by explaining that to Jermaine "rules just don't mean much yet." Now Derek reminds Sean of their conversation, knowing that Sean will need help to hold on to that perspective. Furthermore, Derek knows that Sean's intense nature makes it harder for him to remember.

Finally, Derek moves the boys beyond their anger and frustration, basing his actions on other values important to him, such as the boys' sense of competency and self-esteem. ·

"Can you two think of a way of playing the game where you don't need to follow rules? Or could you think of something else to play that you both can enjoy?"

Teaching values is a process that goes on daily. To be able to integrate their values into their parenting as they did, Derek and Bianca showed they *knew* what their values were. They knew they wanted their children to be able to care, to know their feelings, to feel competent and good about themselves. They also saw opportunities to *apply* their values. Derek did not tell the boys how to play the game together, but left it up to them to figure that out. His suggestion implied that the boys were competent enough to do this.

Derek also listened. He reminded Sean about Jermaine's understanding of rules. He also knew that Sean's comprehension and behavior were more influenced by his developmental level and his temperament than by his parents' values. Derek and Bianca knew what information and skills their boys would need in order to be able to live by values such as caring for others. Sean, and eventually his brother, would need to be able to learn about a situation and to understand another's point of view.

Below is an analysis of the value *caring,* such as Derek and Bianca would have done. This kind of analysis is very helpful in thinking through what the value actually means to you, what knowledge and skills you (or a child) need in order to be able to live by the value, and what the developmental steps are in achieving the ability to do so. It also includes consideration of how other characteristics, such as needs, temperament patterns, and learning style affect how you teach the value.

Analyzing a Value

Caring, able to care

Thinking about the value

Definition: Able to feel, think, and act in the interests of others, oneself, and the environment

Behavior reflecting value: He picks up litter by the side of the road; fixes a snack willingly for a younger sibling; reads to an elderly neighbor whose eyesight is failing. He refuses to take drugs. He makes sure pets have food, water, exercise, and shelter.

Knowledge and skills needed: He can brainstorm ideas. He can recognize the need for relevant knowledge and skills, and has the ability to seek them out. He has the skills needed to put caring into action. He can make decisions based on caring as a value, and he can plan and carry out his plan.

Insights about the value: Behaving in a caring way relies heavily on wanting to do so and having the appropriate information and skills. Decision-making skills are particularly important.

Value present at birth?___Yes __X_No

Teaching or preserving the value

Baby: Teach him to differentiate between living and nonliving things. Help him interact with other people. Help him experience consequences in the natural world by providing safe opportunities, such as having him hold something very warm while you say "hot."

Toddler: Provide opportunities for him to be around other people, including babies and other toddlers. Help him learn that humans must be touched differently from objects, that they cry and can be hurt, and that they are particularly fun to be with.

Preschool: Help him learn to take turns and then to share, and that others have feelings similar to his own. Continue to provide opportunities for him to interact with other people. Give him a chance to entertain a younger child and to care for the environment (picking up trash at the playground or while taking a walk, for example).

School age: Encourage him to recognize the need for information about what he is going to care for—younger child, pet, plant, etc.—and the need for skills to put his caring into action. Teach him how to get information and skills. Help him understand how another person may think and feel differently than he does. Talk about how people differ and how their needs differ as a result. Discuss how to plan to care for a younger child for a short time, maybe by reading a story or playing a game. Talk about how to care for the environment.

Teenage: Provide opportunities for him to care for something. By this age he should be able to be involved, take another's perspective, find out the needs of the person or thing being cared for, understand the situation, and make plans. He should possess skills to put caring into action or know how to acquire them. If he does not have the skills, which is very possible given that our culture does not emphasize caring, you may need to provide opportunities for him to learn. **Note:** Developmental tasks of teenagers frequently interfere with the ability to care for other people or things. On the other hand, teenagers are often the most altruistic of people.

Influences on learning the value

Needs: His social needs will provide some motivation for him to want to learn how to care for others, including pets.

Temperament: If he is emotionally sensitive, he will be aware of how another is feeling, which gives him useful information when he wants to care for another person. A child who is very focused on his own affairs and is not a strong "people" person has more difficulty thinking about the needs of others.

Learning style: A visual learner needs visual clues, so books, pictures, and charts are helpful in teaching what is involved in caring for someone or something, like a pet.

Reflections about the value

Influence of other values: Thoughtful decision making is important in dealing with a situation in which we plan to care for someone or something. Information and relevant skills are necessary. A child needs to learn when it is appropriate to care and when it is more important to base his behavior on other values, such as assertiveness, competitiveness, or attention to his own needs.

New thinking resulting from analysis: Acting in a caring way requires more than the simple desire to be helpful. It is a complex process, requiring motivation, knowledge, and skills.

Parents who are unaware of their values are apt to miss opportunities to teach them, or to be inconsistent in their teaching. Thinking back to the example of Suzy and her grandmother, we can see that parents who have not figured out all their values might be concerned most about the grandmother's feelings, perceiving Suzy's reaction as rude. On the other hand, if another child had given the teddy bear to Suzy, they might be more inclined to respond to Suzy and her disappointment. It would be easy to miss the opportunity to help the child be aware of her feelings as well as the other person's *and* still learn how to deal with the situation.

This book guides you as you address all the challenges raised above. *Stories* expanded from real-life experiences illustrate how parents can identify and define their values and integrate them into family life. *Descriptions* discuss the process. *Content* gives background about how needs, developmental levels, learning styles, and temperaments impact children's abilities to learn and live by the values parents choose. *Examples* demonstrate how values must be analyzed to make them relevant to everyday family life. *Exercises* guide parents through the process of identifying their values, defining them, and analyzing what children need to be able to do to live by the selected values. Parents who complete these exercises will have a guide for integrating their values into their family life.

2

What Are Your Values?

Values can be guides to living, as they are for Derek and Bianca. They can provide a powerful means of influencing children in the ways you wish them to grow. Yet parents seldom think about what their values are, and they are seldom asked.

IDENTIFY YOUR VALUES

To get the most out of this book, you will need to think through what values you want your child to live by 10 to 30 years from now. What behaviors do you want to see? Do you want your child to be responsible? Able to meet the expectations set by having a job? Do you want him to be caring? Able to form lasting, caring relationships? Do you want her to feel connected? Able to see the connectedness and beauty of life?

This book offers you four methods for identifying your values. You may list your values right out (page 20). You may choose your values from a list of possible attributes (page 21). You may find your values by thinking in terms of behavior (page 24): "I want my child to be/do . . ." The fourth way is to write a narrative of your values, a sort of thinking-aloud process in which you talk about what you value and why (page 32). Choose the way that stimulates your thinking. It is not necessary to do all four ways.

YOUR PERSONAL VALUES GUIDE

Parents (and others who work with children) who want to base their parenting on values must know what is involved in living by each of their values: what they are and mean; when relevant behavior appears in a child; what information and skills are needed.

To help you gather information and think about these issues related to values, there is a "Family Guide to Parenting with Values in Mind" at the back of the book (page 164). Completing the relevant parts of the worksheet entitled "Analyzing a Value" as you read this book will add substantially to your ability to integrate your values into your family life. When you have completed the entire "Guide" you will have a handy reference to guide you as your children grow.

To begin writing your own guide, list on page 165 the values you have identified after completing the exercise(s) that follow. Also, write each individual value on its own "Analyzing a Value" worksheet, pages166–167. Make as many copies of this two-page form as you need.

Identifying My Values

Write down fifteen to twenty qualities that you consider to be the most important ones for a person to exhibit in his or her behavior. *These are your values.* Examples: industrious, honest, assertive

_____   _____

_____   _____

_____   _____

_____   _____

_____   _____

_____   _____

_____   _____

_____   _____

_____   _____

_____   _____

Using a List of Attributes to Identify My Values

1. Check all the qualities you would like to see in your child 10 to 30 years from now. Add attributes you want that are not here. If you have more than one child, select attributes for each child by using different colored pens.

2. Circle the fifteen to twenty attributes that are the *most important* to you. (Several terms may describe the same attribute. Pick the one term that best represents the value as a whole to you.) *These are your values.*

Accepting	Careful	Contented
Accurate	Caring	Conventional
Active	Cautious	Cooperative
Adaptable	Cheerful	Courageous
Adventurous	Clean/neat	Courteous
Affectionate	Clear-thinking	Creative
Aggressive	Clever	Critical
Alert	Coherent	Curious
Altruistic	Committed	Daring
Ambitious	Common sense,	Decisive
Amusing	have	Dedicated
Anticipate,	Communicative	Deliberate
able to	Community-oriented	Demanding
Argumentative	Compassionate	Democratic
Artistic	Competent	Dependable
Assertive	Competitive	Determined
Athletic	Complete plans,	Dignified
Attractive	able to	Diligent
Authoritative	Compliant	Discerning
Autonomous	Confident	Discreet
Aware	Conforming	Dominating
Bold	Connected	Eager
Broad-minded	Conscientious	Easy-going
Businesslike	Conservative	Ecologically
Calm	Considerate	concerned
Capable	Consistent	Effective

Efficient
Emotional
Empathic
Encouraging
Energetic
Enterprising
Enthusiastic
Ethical
Expressive
Fair-minded
Faithful
Family-oriented
Farsighted
Fatherly
Feminine
Firm
Flexible
Forceful
Forgiving
Formal
Frank
Friendly
Frugal
Fun-loving
Generous
Gentle
Genuine
Giving
Good judgment,
    have
Good-natured
Happy
Happy-go-lucky
Hardworking
Healthy
Helpful
Honest

Humorous
Idealistic
Imaginative
Independent
Individualistic
Industrious
Informal
Ingenious
Initiative, have
Inquisitive
Insightful
Integrated
Integrity, have
Intellectual
Intelligent
Interested
Intuitive
Inventive
Involved
Jolly
Joyful
Kind
Knowledgeable
Laid back
Liberal
Light-hearted
Likable
Logical
Loving
Loyal
Masculine
Mature
Methodical
Meticulous
Mild
Moderate
Modest

Moral
Motherly
Nature-loving
Natural
Nurturing
Obedient
Obliging
Open
Opportunistic
Optimistic
Orderly
Organized
Original
Other-centered
Outgoing
Painstaking
Patient
Patriotic
Peaceful
Perceptive
Perfectionistic
Persistent
Plan,
    able to
Playful
Pleasant
Poised
Polite
Popular
Practical
Precise
Problem solve,
    able to
Progressive
Proud
Prudent
Purposeful

Quick
Quiet
Rational
Realistic
Reasonable
Reflective
Relaxed
Reliable
Religious
Reserved
Resourceful
Respectful
Responsible
Responsive
Robust
Self-aware
Self-centered
Self-confident
Self-controlled
Self-disciplined
Self-driving
Self-educating
Self-esteeming
Self-fulfilling
Self-motivating
Self-reliant
Self-respecting
Self-restrained
Self-sufficient
Sensible
Sensitive
Serious
Sharp-witted
Sincere
Skillful
Sociable
Sophisticated

Spiritual
Spontaneous
Spunky
Stable
Steady
Strong
Strong convictions,
    have
Strong-minded
Sympathetic
Tactful
Talkative
Teachable
Tenacious
Tender
Thirsty for
    knowledge
Thorough
Thoughtful
Tolerant
Tough
Trusting
Trustworthy
Truthful
Unaffected
Unassuming
Uncritical
Understanding
Uninhibited
Verbal
Versatile
Warm
Well-informed
Well-mannered
Wholesome
Yielding
Zealous

Using Behaviors to Identify My Values

Choose twenty examples that *represent* behaviors you most want to see in your child 10 to 30 years from now. *The corresponding attributes listed on the opposite page are your values.* Example: Someone who greets a child with a hug or holds hands with his or her spouse can be described as affectionate. *Affectionate* is a value.

Adult behavior reflecting value

☐ Greets child with a big hug.
☐ Holds hands with spouse.

☐ Is the first to state opinion about a political leader.
☐ Tells people around her when she needs time to be alone.

☐ Listens to both sides of the argument, then makes up own mind.
☐ Decides when it is time to change jobs.

☐ Notices argument starting between siblings.
☐ Perceives joy of reserved child invited to go to the zoo.

☐ Mows the lawn for a disabled neighbor.
☐ Takes a garbage bag along on walks to pick up trash.

☐ Takes children on the outing as promised.
☐ Shows up for weekly telephone crisis line counseling.

☐ Listens to a child, reflects her view and feelings about a problem.
☐ Gives a clear description of policy changes to employees.

☐ Knows what to do when a child injures himself.
☐ Can figure out how the model airplane works.

☐ Plays best when other team is very good.
☐ Always aims to outsell fellow sales associates.

Note: The horizontal lines running across the facing pages exist only to help you read across the two pages. They have no other significance.

Attribute	Definition
Affectionate	Feels warmly toward others.
Assertive	Speaks and acts without hesitation.
Autonomous	Thinks and acts independently.
Aware	Notices what is going on around her.
Caring	Acts in the interests of others.
Committed	Follows through on pledges.
Communicative	Gives and receives information accurately.
Competent	Is capable; has skills.
Competitive	Likes rivalry.

Adult behavior reflecting value

☐ Follows spouse's vacation plans without comment.
☐ Allows others to break in line ahead of her.

☐ Enjoys the four-year-old's account of his day's adventures.
☐ Sees bugs and plants as living things; doesn't step on them.

☐ Checks that the diaper bag has toys, a snack, and clean diapers.
☐ Follows through to resolve a customer's complaint.

☐ Is pleased with his home, job, and family.
☐ Feels she has enough of everything she needs.

☐ Agrees to bring a salad for the party and helps clean up afterwards.
☐ Plans with others how to run the school auction.

☐ Speaks out about illegal or immoral practices.
☐ Intervenes when someone is being bullied.

☐ Devises an engrossing activity for children on a rainy day.
☐ Discovers a way to recycle used motor oil.

☐ Gets on the Internet to find out why the bees are dying.
☐ Takes an old car apart to figure out how it runs.

☐ Feels the pain of the young child who loses at "Fish."
☐ Sends money to the Red Cross to help flood and earthquake victims.

☐ Enjoys wrestling with the children at the end of a busy day.
☐ Is involved in many activities and always on the go.

☐ Does not take supplies home from the office.
☐ Tells child when she is leaving, instead of sneaking out.

☐ Is willing to bike or take the bus to work if car is in use.
☐ Enjoys fancy parties as well as camping trips.

Attribute	Definition
Compliant	Conforms or yields to others.
Connected	Feels a relationship to people and the world.
Conscientious	Plans and works thoughtfully.
Contented	Feels satisfied with what she has.
Cooperative	Can work with others.
Courageous	Stands up for convictions.
Creative/ imaginative	Thinks of new ways of doing things.
Curious	Likes to investigate; figure out things.
Empathic	Feels as others are feeling.
Energetic	Has energy to spare.
Ethical	Acts from a personal moral code.
Flexible	Responds according to circumstance.

Adult behavior reflecting value

☐ Smiles readily at people.
☐ Talks to people easily about their lives and concerns.

☐ Moves over and slows down to let the tailgating car pass.
☐ Does not allow small children to be unsupervised.

☐ Enjoys a day filled with physical activity.
☐ Seldom catches other people's colds.

☐ Chuckles at toddlers pulling on the same truck, shrieking, "Share!"
☐ Laughs when fooled by a practical joke.

☐ Weeds the garden after a day at the office.
☐ Paints the house in time to avoid the coming bad weather.

☐ Sees the visiting boy's embarrassment over spilling his milk.
☐ Recognizes the common goals of the two rival groups.

☐ Can see the pros and cons of several vacation ideas.
☐ Able to find and compare information about her mother's illness.

☐ Keeps in touch regularly with all her family members.
☐ Volunteers to read to sick children at the hospital.

☐ Knows all there is to know about the state of Alaska.
☐ Advises others on the legal requirements of wills and trusts.

☐ Recognizes the week ahead will be very busy and freezes extra meals.
☐ Schedules two meetings in the same part of town on Tuesday.

☐ Gets three children to different, simultaneous soccer games on time.
☐ Figures out how to get respite care for self and disabled child.

☐ Reviews the circumstances when the child had a tantrum.
☐ Compares his spending to his financial obligations.

Attribute	*Definition*
Friendly	Shows kindly interest and goodwill.
Good judgment	Makes wise decisions.
Healthy	Has a sound body and mind.
Humorous	Is funny; can appreciate a joke.
Industrious	Works hard.
Insightful	Aware of the inner nature of something.
Intelligent	Able to think complexly.
Involved	Knows and participates in activity.
Knowledgeable	Has breadth of information.
Plans ahead	Seeks ways to achieve an end.
Problem solver	Finds workable solutions.
Reflective	Thinks over, reviews.

Adult behavior reflecting value

☐ Responds to a child's request for help with a smile and a nod.
☐ Does not make comments about anyone's unusual appearance.

☐ Obeys traffic laws.
☐ Takes care of personal belongings and honors commitments.

☐ Sympathizes with friend's anguish over death of parent.
☐ Enjoys with the child her delight in sparkling soap bubbles.

☐ Knows when she's tired and needs to change activities.
☐ Knows when he's getting angry or upset.

☐ Feels capable of getting around a new city successfully.
☐ Is sure he can perform well on the softball team.

☐ Functions effectively in a medical emergency.
☐ Responds calmly when confronted with road rage.

☐ Gathers information about plants that attract butterflies.
☐ Uses prep time for a professional exam to extend knowledge.

☐ Plans enough time to exercise before going to work.
☐ Clears the vacant lot of garbage to create a safe place for play.

☐ Takes responsibility for medical and dental check-ups yearly.
☐ Can get around the city alone in his wheelchair.

☐ Can change the car's flat tire.
☐ Can mediate between two groups who are in disagreement.

☐ Believes others when they say they will do something.
☐ Feels certain that no one will harm her.

☐ Honors promise to visit homebound friend regularly.
☐ Handles the money paid into the company honestly.

Attribute	Definition
Respectful	Shows regard for another person.
Responsible	Answers for own conduct.
Responsive	Relates with feeling to people.
Self-aware	Knows personal feelings and acts.
Self-confident	Feels able to do things; sure of self.
Self-controlled	Controls own behavior.
Self-educating	Seeks out information and skills.
Self-motivating	Able to get on with what needs to be done.
Self-reliant	Able to take care of self.
Skillful	Competent at tasks.
Trusting	Has confidence in others.
Trustworthy	Is worthy of others' confidence.

Identifying My Values by Thinking Through What Is Important to Me

1. Read this *example* of a parent writing a narrative about what she wants in her life.
2. Then write a paragraph or more about what is important to you in your life and what you hope for the lives of your children.
3. When you have finished writing, go through and underline the qualities or attributes you have identified and make a list of them. *These are your values.*

୧୬

I want to live a fulfilling life, and I want that for my children, too. A fulfilling life includes deep, satisfying relationships with a partner, friends, children, and parents. It includes work that demands excellence, that stretches one's thinking and skills, and that contributes to the society in which we live. It means being a contributing member of the community. A fulfilling life deepens one's spiritual understanding and has room for aesthetic experiences.

To be able to live such a life and to prepare my children, I must consider the kind of world in which we find ourselves or they might find themselves. It could be a world with minimal resources, especially of energy. It could be a world flooded with new sources of energy not easily imaginable today. It could be a world at war or one in which peaceful methods of solving conflict have been found. Not knowing the kind of world that my children may live in makes it important for them to be able to be *flexible* and to *solve problems.* They must be able to search for alternative lifestyles.

My values will allow me to live such a life and prepare my children for theirs.

Having an abundance of *energy* will certainly facilitate meeting the challenge of living a fulfilling life, regardless of the kind of world in which we find ourselves. Having energy assumes being *healthy.* Being engaged with what is happening is also another requirement. My definition of a fulfilling life is not a monastic one, but one of being *involved.*

To be able to deal with the uncertainty of the kind of world in which we may live, to know who is around us and what they may be feeling, being *aware* of our surroundings is an absolute necessity. Being aware will give us some of the information we need to search for new answers. We will also need to know how to search out information; we need to be *self-educating*.

The knowledge that we find will help us *solve problems,* be reflective, find answers. We will be *creative.* In making our decisions, we will take into consideration their effect on the people around us, the environment, and ourselves. Our planning will be guided by our *caring* for all three, our ethical code. And we will be both *autonomous* and *self-confident* enough that we can live by the answers that we find. We will move ahead; we will have *initiative.*

To find fulfillment in relationships means being able to be *affectionate* with others and to be *cooperative* when working with them.

To find fulfillment in work requires being willing to work, being *industrious,* and having the relevant skills, being *competent.*

Living and contributing to the community requires having an ethical standard and a commitment to it that may be based on a feeling of being *connected.*

In spite of all the change and uncertainty, there is a *trust* in others, ourselves, and our world that the world works according to a plan. We can search for that plan and through it we gain a sense of *integrity.*

Finally, we greet all the change and uncertainty, the sameness and routine, the challenges with their triumphs and disappointments with a *sense of humor,* being able to see the funny side of an issue.

List of values named

affectionate	creative	involved
autonomous	energy/energetic	problem solver
aware	flexible	self-confident
caring	healthy	self-educating
competent	industrious	sense of humor
connected	initiative	trusting/trustworthy
cooperative	integrity	

What do your values
mean to you?

Now that you have identified your values, you need to know exactly what they mean to you. Names of values can have many different meanings, as any dictionary illustrates. Caring can mean liking someone and having a crush on someone. It can also mean providing for the needs of someone or something (Grandpa, a pet, the garden, for example). Caring can also mean knowing, feeling, and acting in the interests of others.

Language is rich in subtle nuances of meaning, and two people can use the same words, but have different interpretations of their meaning. To be able to use values in parenting consistently and effectively, you have to know what you mean.

Ron, Lois, Maria, and several other parents meet once a week in a parenting discussion group. In this evening's session they are considering their values and struggling to come to an understanding of the words they use to name their values.

Ron began, "I want my daughter to be healthy. I want her to be physically strong with lots of energy. Not really an Olympic champion, but able to enjoy sports."

"I selected that value, too," laughed Lois, "but I was thinking of Jennifer's being mentally healthy, having lots of psychic energy and being able to think ahead and not be overcome with worry."

"Identifying my values wasn't easy," picked up Maria. "I felt so torn. I want my daughter to be assertive. She's going to have to stand up for herself in the work place. She's going to have to say clearly what she feels and thinks and be able to take care of herself. On the other hand, I don't want Josh to be assertive. He pushes his way in too much already. He interrupts. He walks into the middle of children playing with blocks and takes over the project without a thought to the other kids' plans. Is it all right to want a value for one child, but not the other?"

"Or maybe," Lois reflected, "you want a value to be shown in certain circumstances. Don't you want Josh to be able to stand up for himself and so on, but at the same time you want him to keep a rein on his assertiveness sometimes? Wouldn't you want that for your daughter, too?"

"Yeah," Maria nodded. "It's almost as if other values, such as being considerate, affect my value of being assertive."

"I found the whole process difficult, too, but for a different reason," Ron broke in. "There were so many choices on the long list of values. To narrow them down to fifteen or twenty seemed impossible until I realized that many of them could be grouped together. Grouping similar attributes helped me clarify my values. I finally chose 'make thoughtful decisions' because that value covers all the others, like clear thinker, being reflective, intelligent, having good judgment, and anticipating consequences."

ᕦᕤ

You can see that these parents were using two of the ways you may have used to clarify the meanings of their values. One was a value's definition. Ron described being healthy as being physically strong, while Lois described it as being mentally fit. The other way all three parents defined a value was by describing the behavior they expected to see in a person having that value. A healthy person "enjoys sports"; an assertive person "stands up for herself." They also observed that behavior based on a value could be inappropriate at times, as shown by Josh's behavior among the children playing with blocks.

DEFINE YOUR VALUES

Write what each value means to you on its own "Analyzing a Value" worksheet (make copies of pages 166–167). If you wish, look up each value in the dictionary and add further clarification. It often helps to talk with another person as you go through this process, just as the parents in the discussion group above were doing. Adapt the definition of each of your values to the behavior you want to see in your children, as Ron did when he emphasized "thoughtful" decision making.

Write examples of some behaviors you accept as showing your values on your worksheets. These can vary from person to person, even when two people say they hold the same values. If intelligence is the value, any of these behaviors might be expected: scores high on an IQ test; can think abstractly about a subject or issue; is a clear, logical thinker; has a large and complex vocabulary; has the ability to outwit business partners; can get out of responsibilities through creative thought and action. It is also helpful sometimes to list situations in which you would not want to see a particular value acted upon.

Remember that it is impossible to apply your values to parenting in an effective way if you do not know what they mean to you. You will find your efforts to define your values now paying off handsomely in the future as you integrate your values into your parenting.

How Do Children Acquire Values?

In the next parenting discussion group, Ron, Lois, and Maria continued the challenge of defining what their values mean, and how these values might affect their children.

Ron reflected, "The funny thing is that clarifying a value's meaning helped me in my parenting. I've always wanted smart kids who could make good decisions. But thinking about 'thoughtful' decisions made me realize there is a process to making good decisions that my kids don't know. They do such stupid things sometimes! Al, for instance, is forever borrowing against his allowance. He's always in debt.

"This week he asked to borrow money to buy a snowboard. It was quite expensive, and he would have been broke for several weeks with no allowance. Rather than tell him it was a stupid idea, which I usually do, I realized he needed to figure out that for himself.

"So I encouraged him to find out how much the thing cost, including the tax. Then we figured out how long it would take him to repay the loan. We used a calendar, so that we could see what things he had planned that might require money. He saw the consequences, and I think the process helped him understand. I noticed that he helped his younger brother figure out the consequence of his wanting something."

Maria turned to Ron with a smile, "That's a wonderful example, Ron. You really took Al through the process of making a thoughtful decision.

"It makes me think of something I've been struggling with. Kids aren't born 'thoughtful' in any meaningful way. They have to learn the skill, just as you were describing. You demonstrated a way to teach them.

"But maybe not all values have to be taught. As I said, I want my children to be assertive. It looks like I don't need to worry about my son—Josh has been assertive since birth! He knows what he wants, when he

wants it, and has no trouble letting everyone else know. With my daughter it's different. Are some values present at birth and some not? If we looked at our kids closely, would we find that they may already be behaving in some ways as we would like, according to our values?"

Lois answered, "That makes sense to me. All kids are born curious, for instance. If our child has the behavior we want, then we can relax. If he doesn't, then we have to figure out a way to teach him how to become whatever it is that we value."

"It's not quite that simple," Maria countered. "Josh is assertive. However, he still needs to learn how to be assertive with consideration for others around him. So my challenge is to help him be aware of other children, but not squelch his assertiveness."

"You want him to be a caring person, as well as assertive?" Ron concluded thoughtfully.

"Yes, that's right," Maria nodded.

These parents brought up several important ideas for parents attempting to use their values to guide parenting decisions. Let us look at each in turn.

VALUES REFLECTED AT BIRTH

Children from birth may be happy, easy-going, and energetic; almost all are born curious. Maria's son was assertive. These behaviors may already reflect values you hold. Look again at your descriptions of each of your values. Check on your "Analyzing a Value" worksheets (page 166 and your copies) which of your values you would expect to see at birth or soon thereafter (say, within a year). *These attributes are part of your child's nature.* They may be strong enough to withstand the rigors of life, no matter what, or you may simply need to watch that they are not lost as your child grows and encounters the world around her.

VALUES MAY NEED TO BE TAUGHT

Parents and other adults usually need to teach those values that children's behavior does not show early in life. Ron concluded this about thoughtful decision making when he analyzed his value of "smart." Similarly, new-born babies are not able to care. They cannot think, feel, or act with concern for another person or thing. Neither can they solve problems or show good judgment. The ability to base one's life on these particular values comes later as the child grows and has opportunities to learn how.

Ron had to analyze what is involved in thoughtful decision making. He figured out that there is a process that includes gathering information about a situation (cost including tax, size of allowance), analyzing the situation (how long to pay back borrowed money), brainstorming possible solutions, and deciding what to do. Ron took Al through this process, a step in Al's learning how to live according to the value of making thoughtful decisions. The analysis of "Makes thoughtful decisions" on page 42 includes this information.

Sean and Jermaine's parents, Derek and Bianca (chapter one), were also making decisions based on a value that had to be taught, how to care. They saw as part of the ability to care the need to recognize the situation, which meant they had to help Sean understand that his brother understood the game differently than he did.

You can tell what a child needs to learn in order to behave according to a value by looking at the behaviors that reflect that value. *What information and skills does a person need in order to be able to behave in a way that reflects that value?* Deciding this for each of your values will give you a list of the skills and information your children need. Record this information for each of your values on your "Analyzing a Value" worksheets (page 166 and your copies).

Children need time to learn and practice skills. Their ability to learn is tied to their developmental stage as well. Sometimes a parent has to wait patiently until a child is ready to learn. For example, knowing that there are different ways to handle situations is a major part of the ability to make thoughtful decisions. Yet, a two-year-old can only make a choice between two options suggested by the parent, and the child usually needs to *see* the two choices. Thinking is closely related to what one can see, hear, and manipulate at this stage of development. Threes and older can *think up* options. Parents frequently have to wait until their children are teenagers to see them able to delay gratification of immediate needs. Even then, because of developmental issues, it may be hard for them to give up a favorite activity in favor of homework, or chores, or other responsibilities.

VALUES CAN BE LOST

Maria brought up another important point when she noted that she did not want to destroy one value (assertiveness) in order to get another (caring). Values can be lost. *Behaviors based on a value must be cherished, protected, and encouraged* even though they have to be modified throughout a person's life.

All children are born curious, for instance. If you value curiosity, you will give your toddler as much space as possible to wander, to explore, to handle things. He or she must be able to experiment with how things work and allowed to make messes of all kinds with mud, clay, water, play dough, objects of all kinds, and more, even though these activities result in more work for you. You will help your older child find out about things, maybe dinosaurs or the Olympic Games, by going to the library with her or getting on the Internet or talking to people who know. She will need to learn to use these resources on her own, too. You will support your teenager who wants to know what it is like to live on his own in the wilderness. Think about how you will support the values that you recognize are already present in your child.

VALUES MAY BE IN CONFLICT

Maria struggled with another idea. She realized that *behaviors based on values can interfere with each other.* Her son Josh's assertiveness was interfering with his ability to be considerate of other children. This potential for conflict can undermine a parent's best efforts if it is not taken into account and dealt with. We will look at this challenge in depth in chapter nine, about resolving conflicting values.

Look at "Analyzing a Value" below to see how to think through what a child needs to learn to be able to make thoughtful decisions.

Analyzing a Value

MAKES THOUGHTFUL DECISIONS

Thinking about the value

Definition: Makes careful, considerate choices

Behavior reflecting value: Makes a schedule for doing her homework based on how much she has, how hard it is, and when she is most alert. Decides whether or not she can afford to buy something based on funds available and other plans that require money.

Knowledge and skills needed: She can describe a situation accurately and knows what other information might be relevant and how to find it. She can brainstorm several options. She can recognize that goals, circumstances, and other considerations may have an impact on her decision, and she can analyze her options based on these.

Insights about the value: Making thoughtful decisions is a process that involves knowing what the situation is, being aware of what the choices are, and having guides to help with making the decision. Development of the ability to make thoughtful decisions will be closely linked to a child's mental development.

Value present at birth?___Yes _X_No

Teaching or preserving the value

Baby: Accept baby's signal that she is full. Recognize her ways of telling you she is tired or wet.

Toddler: Encourage her to make simple decisions, such as to have one apple slice or two. Show her the items as that will help her to choose. Teach her the words to describe choices.

Preschool: Help her describe a situation. Encourage her to think of two or three alternatives. Help her make choices in regard to social situations.

Point out that it is more fun to play dress-up with another person than to play alone.

School age: Help her gather information about a situation. This may mean a trip to the library or exploring the Internet. Encourage her to think of several options. Have her make decisions, accepting the fact that they will be based on absolutes. At this stage of development, something is either right or wrong; there are no gray areas.

Teenage: Allow and encourage her to describe a situation with accuracy, think of many options, accumulate a fund of information on which to base a decision, analyze situations and options, and make a choice based on the information she has.

Influences on learning the value

Needs: Her curiosity is a strong motivator for the development of this ability.

Temperament: If she is an impulsive child who is frequently highly distractible and persistent, it will be hard for her to stop and anticipate consequences of action. However, learning to make thoughtful decisions may help her become less impulsive.

Learning style: If her preferred learning style is visual, for instance, she will find problem solving easier if visual clues, such as lists, pictures, and graphs, are provided and she is shown how to do something.

Reflections about the value

Influence of other values: Being aware is a value that impacts making thoughtful decisions. The more aware a child is of her environment, the people in it and what they are doing, saying, and feeling, the objects in the environment, and what is happening, the more information she will have on which to base her decisions.

New thinking resulting from analysis: It is amazing at what a young age children can start to learn to make decisions. They can think of choices, choose certain ones, and see the results of their choices in their play as early as two years old. Making thoughtful decisions is a process, not an instant event, and parents need to be patient with the learning.

Recognizing how values differ is necessary in order to integrate them realistically into family life. Behavior related to a value that is present at birth (such as curiosity) must be guarded and cherished. In contrast, parents must plan when to teach behavior related to a value that must be learned (such as caring).

Values do not stand alone. One can support another. Being able to make thoughtful decisions helps a person to be more caring, for example. One value can conflict with another, also. In our culture, a feminine woman who is assertive and a masculine man who is in touch with his feelings are contradictions in terms.

Two sections in "Analyzing a Value" give you a chance to think about the interactions of values and other factors that influence their use, "Insights about the value" and "Reflections about the value." Giving thought to the implications of the values you hold will put you in a stronger position to live by your values.

Reflecting on Family Life

• Name a value you find yourself working to preserve in your child.
• Describe your plan for doing this.
• Name a value of yours that your child needs information and skills to be able to do.
• Describe your plan for helping your child learn what he or she needs.

4

Values Can
Guide Family Life

Parents integrate values into family life situation by situation by situation. All kinds of situations provide opportunities to do this: planning a summer vacation, dealing with squabbling siblings, struggling over unfinished homework, getting a family pet, potty training, feeding the baby, teaching the teenager to drive. . . .

Nina had accepted a new, full-time job outside the home starting in the fall. She and her husband Tad knew that this was going to be a big change for their family of three children, Joel, 14, Monique, 9, and Liz, 4. Tad immediately saw the change as an opportunity to integrate some of their values as they had been learning how to do in the parenting discussion group.

"This will be a chance to have the kids take on more responsibility for household chores around here. With you home they've really not had to pitch in very much," he observed.

"I know," responded Nina. "Sometimes it's just easier to do the work myself. The question is, how can we get the kids to help?"

"Well, we could just tell them to get busy and help . . . as if that would work," added Tad with a chuckle.

"Or put up a list and let them choose which chores they want to do," Nina said doubtfully.

Or we could assign the chores."

"We could set a certain day of the week, like Saturday morning, when all chores have to be done."

"Or let them do their chores when they wanted to."

"Maybe we should say when, though, like dishes done before going to bed or certain chores done on the weekend."

"The kids could even make up the list of what has to be done."

"But we'd better have a complete list in our pockets to be sure they didn't forget something."

"Or we could have a family meeting, tell them about your job and what that'll mean for the family, then ask them how they think we should handle chores."

"Then we could ask them how they want to assign jobs."

"But I think we need to keep some control . . . have some say. I can see Liz choosing to mow the lawn, which she's too little to do."

"We could ask the kids about fairness after everyone's signed up."

"Well, we have lots of choices," said Nina, looking at the list. "Several of them involve thinking. This is a good time to have the kids do some practical thinking about a problem. We value problem solving. Having them list what needs to be done would reinforce the idea that you need to know what you're talking about when you want to solve a problem."

"Yes, having them do that and having each of them decide which chores they'll do should give their egos a boost. . . . 'Mom and Dad trust me to make this decision.' Besides, I think they'll be more cooperative. I know when I'm working, having some choice about when and where makes me more cooperative," observed Tad.

"So, having a family meeting would be a good place to start. Then we'd all be working together. It'd give a spirit of cooperation to this effort," said Nina.

"We've made a plan! And I like it. I feel good when our plan rests on our values. We'll have a family meeting and talk about your job. We'll have everyone work together to make a list of chores that need to be done. Then everyone can choose their chores and decide when they'll do them," concluded Tad.

"With us reserving the right to question fairness, no one doing more that his or her share. Oh, also the right to decide by what time chores must be done," cautioned Nina.

The family gathered the next Friday evening. Together Tad and Nina told the children about Nina's job. They described the changes that would have to take place to get household chores done. They were amazed at how complete the list of chores was that they all drew up together. The volunteering for chores did not go as smoothly. Tad and Nina felt that Joel wasn't taking his fair share. Joel felt that Liz was getting off too easy. Everyone agreed to keep track of the time each chore took as one way to judge whether or not the distribution of chores was fair.

On reflection, Nina and Tad felt they had given their children an opportunity to learn what was involved in planning who would be responsible for which family chores. They also felt that on the whole the children had accepted the idea of their new responsibilities. The question was, would they follow through? Whether they did or not, Tad and Nina still felt that having a family meeting over something involving everyone was a good way to deal with issues, as well as a method to remember for future problem solving. Their values guided how these parents dealt with a situation their family faced.

INTEGRATING VALUES INTO PARENTING

You can pick out in the example above some of the values Nina and Tad held: *thoughtful decision making, being responsible,* and *healthy self-esteem.* These parents planned how to reorganize the family chores based on those three values.

They followed a basic process that you too can use when dealing with most situations in your family. This process, "Parenting with Values in Mind," has three steps:

Step 1. Make a plan. Use your values to decide which ideas to implement.
• Describe a situation in your family that needs attention.
• Brainstorm ideas to deal with the situation.
• Make a plan of what to do about the situation, using your ideas that support your values.

Step 2. Carry out your plan.

Step 3. Reflect on your plan.

On pages 49 and 51 is a full description of how this process works. You will have several opportunities to practice throughout the book.

Parenting with Values in Mind

Step One: Plan

Describe a situation in your family that needs attention.

The situation can exist now, or be one coming up in the future. It could be a time of excitement, or perhaps of stress and sorrow. It can be a small challenge, or a large one. Maybe it has happened before, or maybe it will be new. The first step is to recognize the situation, know details about it, and be able to describe it. What is happening, or going to happen, or often happens? Who is involved? How are they feeling? What has to be done, and when?

Brainstorm—think of as many ideas to deal with the situation as you can.

When you think of ideas, it is fun and productive to work with a partner or friends. The more ideas you have, the better. You would never consider implementing some of the ideas you will collectively think up. Some will be absurd, some impossible, some lame, some funny . . . and some just right, but while you are thinking of them is not the time to judge them. The objective of brainstorming is to think of lots of ideas, as quickly as possible, without deciding right then that something will or will not work.

Make a plan of how to deal with the situation, using your ideas that support your values.

Choose ideas, courses of action, using your values as guides. What values are relevant to the situation? What ideas will you choose based on your values? Do some of your choices provide an opportunity to model one or more of your values? Do they provide opportunities to teach information and skills children need to implement specific values?

Note: Chapters five through eight identify issues that influence how values can be integrated into family life. Glance ahead, if you wish, to the exercises "Parenting with Values in Mind" in each of those chapters to see what new information will be added to your planning process.

Step Two: Carry out your plan

Planning is a waste of time if you do not follow the course of action.

Step Three: Reflect on your plan

Review your plan. What worked well? What values do you feel your children now know more about and can use? What would you do differently next time? Has this particular challenge led to others?

VALUES GUIDE DECISIONS

Values can alert parents to experiences their children need. If you are aware that your child is not demonstrating a value you think important, use a situation to help your child learn, as Keith's parents did below.

Keith had never been interested in his younger brother and sister. He could step right over them and not notice their attempts to get his attention. He gave almost as little attention to his mom and dad. At 12, Keith was a computer whiz. He could always figure out how to make it work when his parents were stumped. He spent hours on the Internet. All his friends talked about at school was computers. The boys never seemed to differentiate between each other. One boy was absent for a week before the group realized he wasn't there. Keith's parents worried about his obliviousness and lack of concern.

"He's too much a loner."

"He's too young to be so wrapped up in something."

"He needs to be more caring. He needs to think about others."

"He needs to be aware of others' needs and even help meet them."

To their surprise, Keith wanted a dog for his birthday. His parents had never wanted a dog because of the trouble and responsibility. However, they saw an opportunity to help Keith become able to care.

Keith's parents had many choices in how to respond to his request. They could just get the dog and let Keith learn what was involved in having a pet. They'd probably end up hassling him about taking care of it.

They could say no. Or they could guide Keith's thinking about what was involved in getting and caring for a dog.

Keith's parents chose the last course of action because they valued caring. They had analyzed what was involved in caring (look back at "Analyzing a Value" on pages 16–17 for an example) and they saw an opportunity to help Keith become more able to care. They asked questions that would encourage Keith to think about what was involved in caring for a dog. What kind of dog did he want? What would be the needs of that kind of dog? Could they provide for those needs where they lived and with the space they had? Could they afford that kind of dog? What did he think he'd like to do with his dog?

When his birthday arrived, Keith had a plan for how he would care for his dog, which was a step in helping him learn to be more caring in general.

Values guide planning

With some thought and determination, you can plan ahead, using your values to guide what you hope the outcome of a situation will be. The two mothers below are struggling with a tough situation and trying to figure out the best way to deal with it.

Roseanne and her sister Lynne were facing the fact that their eighty-four-year-old father was very ill and most likely dying. Even in their sorrow they both knew they would eventually have to deal with their children's reactions. He was a beloved grandfather who had been part of their children's lives. He had attended tea parties, played school, built tree houses, and taught them about carpentry and how to fish. Lynne's children, Beth, 16, Jamie, 13, and Sam, 10, would miss him. Roseanne's children were much younger. Three-month-old Jeff would not remember his granddad nor be aware of the sorrow around him as long as he was fed, changed, and cuddled. But with three-and-a-half-year-old Nancy, the situation was not so easy to deal with.

"The kids are still in school," Lynne began. "They can stay at home in New York and we'll just tell them when Dad dies. They're still so young.

They shouldn't have to deal with this."

"But your kids know him so well, and they're not that young anymore. Don't you want them to come up this weekend to say good-bye?" asked Roseanne.

"That would be so sad," countered her sister. "I'd cry. And I don't know how Beth and Jamie would react. At 16 and 13, one never knows how they will take things."

"Well, I've thought of every way to handle this with Nancy. I've thought about sending her to Jim's folks. I've gotten some books out of the library that talk about death and dying. I've thought about taking her to see Dad. And I've thought about ignoring the whole problem and going on as if nothing were happening, which at the moment is the easiest.

"But Jim made me face the situation last night. He reminded me of how we value being aware. We've worked to keep Nancy aware of everything around her. You remember how alert she was to music while I was still pregnant with her? And she has always taken in so much by looking and listening."

"Yes," smiled Lynne, "including taking 30 minutes to walk the short distance to the mail box last summer at the cabin. She had to greet every mushroom, and there were so many!"

"Right," Roseanne continued, "so Jim argued that we can't deny her awareness of Dad's illness. She knows something's wrong. She keeps asking to see him. We told her that Granddad is very, very ill. Today we're taking her to the hospital to see him. He'll like that. He's still conscious and seeing her will cheer him up. Then we're going to start talking about death so she'll be prepared and can take part in the grieving when it's time. I know I want her to know the emotions and have the words to express how she's feeling. We value keeping her aware of her surroundings and what's happening, and this is the best way we can think to do that."

"Wow!" was Lynne's only response.

Roseanne and Lynne, working out their own feelings, were planning how to guide their children through this time of grief. Their choices ranged from removing the kids from the situation altogether to making them fully aware of and participants in it. Each one finally made her decision based on her own values as she understood them. Roseanne, who had a clearer idea of her values than her sister, decided to let her daughter experience her grandfather's illness and eventual death. Honoring her value of being aware (look at "Analyzing a Value" below), she was going to include Nancy in the events surrounding a beloved grandfather's dying. Lynne, grieving and unclear about her values and unsure about how her children might respond, was leaning toward taking the easiest course, that of waiting until her father died and then telling her children.

Analyzing a Value

AWARE

~~~~~~~~~~

Thinking about the value

Definition: Open to what is going on around one; having intensified perceptions; noticing details

Behavior reflecting value: She notices when someone looks unhappy. She recognizes changes in the landscape. She hears the change in a person's tone of voice. She understands the unspoken meanings in what people say.

Knowledge and skills needed: She must be able to feel, see, hear, touch, and remember.

Insights about the value: A child's awareness can vary from totally unaware to overly sensitive. You have to decide how much awareness needs to be taught, and what kind: beauty of nature? kindness of others? feelings of playmates? You must also decide how to introduce awareness of the unpleasant facts of life, such as starvation, war, violence, effects of natural disasters, etc.

Value present at birth? _X_ Yes ___No

Teaching or preserving the value

Baby: Give her an interesting environment to look at, touch, taste, listen to, and manipulate. Keep her safe as she explores. Give her the words for what she is doing as she does it. Acknowledge her feelings and give her words for feelings, too. Grant her time: time in which to grow and develop as well as time to be with her parents.

Toddler: Give her the same experiences as baby. Provide new opportunities to explore, such as other people's homes, the grocery store, playgrounds, natural areas, the library, Mom or Dad's office. As she becomes able, encourage her to talk about her experiences, what she does, hears, and sees. Give her more words, including abstract ones, such as for feelings.

Preschool and school age: Continue giving opportunities to experience things, with ever widening scope, keeping aware of both her interests and her lack of experience. Support her in those experiences that are sad or tragic for her. Answer her questions with accurate information and discuss issues important to her. Help her learn to find answers for herself.

Teenage: At this stage, she becomes aware of abstract concepts such as ethics, morality, double standards, contradictions between word and deed. Continue to support her exploration and encourage her awareness, even of painful or frightening ideas and experiences.

Influences on learning the value

Needs: An extremely sensitive child's needs to feel safe and protected can be taxing. Be particularly careful not to overburden such a child and help her learn how to deal with her sensitivities. If she is unaware, she can be oblivious to potential danger, so you must work to keep her safe.

Temperament: If she has high sensory awareness, she will be more aware of what is going on around her. Acknowledge her experiences and give her words to describe them. If she is oblivious, coach her and point things out to her, describing what she sees happening.

Learning style: If she has a strong preference for either auditory or visual learning and is also oblivious, teach her in her preferred learning style how to be aware. For example, if she is unaware that her friend wants to play, say, "Julia wants to play with you. See how she has come over to you and is offering to share her toy?"

Reflections about the value

Influence of other values: To be aware requires energy and alertness. A child will need to be healthy, well-nourished, and rested in order to be aware of what is happening around her.

New thinking resulting from analysis: It would be very easy to shut off a child's awareness of what is going on around her by preventing her from exploring and by denying what she experiences. A very aware child could also be easily overwhelmed in today's world.

QUESTIONS ABOUT INTEGRATING VALUES

Warning signals may be flashing for many of you at this point. This monologue may capture your concerns:

"Yes, figuring out my values, thinking them through, and using them to guide my family life sounds fine, but will it work? What about the ages of my kids—maybe they're too young, or maybe it's too late. Won't that make a difference? How can I get my kids interested? Aren't there easier ways to teach values, maybe by reading stories or playing games? Isn't it enough to go to religious services every week?

"What if I have trouble being consistent in what behavior I want from the kids? How do I give clear directions? What can I do about values that seem to contradict each other—like independence vs. obedience? Or honesty vs. politeness? And what in the world do I do with my teenager who questions everything?"

We will consider all these questions in the chapters that follow.

Reflecting on Family Life

• Review in detail what happened in a situation you dealt with recently.
• What values did you use in this situation?
• Were they values that you identified as important to you?
• Brainstorm as many ways as you can think of which you could have used in that situation.

5

Basic Needs Affect Learning

The parenting discussion group met again the following week. The parents were eager to explore other considerations that might affect the use of values to guide their decisions.

"In our house," Lois said "our fourteen-year-old son Steven and I are responsible for cleaning up the kitchen after dinner. I had suggested that he clean three nights a week and I four. Well, that didn't work. Steven moped around, did a lousy job, and complained about all the homework he had. Seems like he always has more homework on his clean-up nights. I want my son to be responsible and do his chores well. And he just wasn't.

"Finally I talked with him. I asked him if he felt our arrangement was working. I told him I didn't like having to check up on him every night. He blurted out how lonely he felt going into that messy kitchen when everyone else was going to do other things.

"So I asked him if he would rather we cleaned the kitchen together, even if he had to do it every evening. He really brightened up at that idea and said, 'Yes!' We've been working together for two weeks now, and he really works. We talk, too. Communication is better than ever!"

Lois has stumbled onto two facts. Many different circumstances present opportunities for passing on (teaching) values, and some circumstances are more effective than others. Steven was more able to assume responsibility for his chores when he worked with his mom than when he worked alone. In chapter four, Nina and Tad decided rightly that by including their children in planning who would do which chores, the children would more easily assume responsibility for their own.

Why? The answer lies in people's needs and the ways that they are or are not satisfied.

WHAT ARE NEEDS?

Needs are demands of the body for physical and psychological well-being. They compel people to find satisfaction. There are six groups of basic needs. If some groups of needs are not met, the person dies: for example, people must have water and food; they must be safe. When these basic needs are not at least partially satisfied, the body's demand becomes all consuming. A starving person cannot think of anything but food.

The satisfaction of other needs makes life rich and fulfilling. Curiosity drives the infant to investigate his world and the astronomer to search the universe. Satisfying that curiosity connects one to life and makes it stimulating and worth living.

The Six Groups of Basic Needs

Group	Need
Physical	For water, food, sleep, shelter, clothing, and reproduction
Protection/Safety	For safe food and water, people, environment, experiences
Social/Affection	To be loved and to love, to feel a part of and to include others
Curiosity/Competence	To know and understand; to be able; to be competent
Self	For self-knowledge, integrity, self-esteem; self-fulfillment; recognition
Aesthetic/Spiritual	For beauty and to create it; for spiritual connectedness

NEEDS AS MOTIVATORS

The body's demands for physical and psychological well-being motivate a person to act and often to change and grow. Nina and Tad understood their children's need to feel competent. They met that need by including the children in the decision about chores, thus making them more likely to assume responsibility for their own. Steven's mother met his social need by washing dishes with him, freeing him to assume responsibility for his chores.

Parents have many choices in how they use their children's needs to encourage their children to grow and change. They can choose which needs they will use. They can choose how they will satisfy these needs.

A parent may choose not to satisfy a need: "You're late. No supper for you." The parent is denying the child's physical need for food.

A parent may postpone satisfaction until the child behaves as expected: "If you don't clean up your room, you can't have Mattie over to play." In this case, the parent is postponing satisfying a social need to make the child complete a task.

A parent may satisfy the child's needs, freeing her to move on with the tasks of learning and growing: "When we spill milk, we need to clean it up," repeats the dad as he hands his toddler a sponge and takes one himself. The parent is satisfying both the child's curiosity about how to accomplish clean-up and her need to feel competent.

WHAT CHILDREN LEARN

Three-year-old Crystal grabbed the doll carriage from her friend Marquita. "I'm going to give my baby a ride," she said. Outraged, Marquita began to cry.

Each of the three responses below encourages Crystal to be considerate of her friend, a step in becoming a caring person. However, each one motivates her by using different needs and, as a consequence, Crystal changes her behavior for different reasons. These reasons influence what she learns.

1. "Stop grabbing!" shouts Crystal's dad as he slaps her hand.
   The need to feel safe will motivate Crystal to refrain from grabbing. She is learning not to grab, at least while her parent is nearby.

2. "If you don't share your toys, you can't play with your friend. I'll take Marquita home," threatens her dad.

   The need to have friends will motivate Crystal to let Marquita use the doll carriage. Crystal will learn that by "sharing" she can have friends visit. She will have little understanding of the relationship between having friends and sharing. She may not even understand what "sharing" means. To a two- or three-year-old it may seem like giving up a toy.

3. "I wonder how you both could give your dolls a ride?" inquired Crystal's dad. The girls came up with several ideas:
   - "We could have our babies sit up."
   - "I could carry my doll and then Marquita could carry hers."
   - "We could both push the doll carriage."
   - "We could take turns. I push the carriage to the porch, Crystal push it back."

In the third example, Dad recognizes the girls' social needs *and* their need to be competent by helping them figure out how to have fun together with the doll carriage. The children are learning that problem solving is a way of dealing with conflicts.

As you see, how needs are satisfied affects what the child learns and is able to do. Children (all people) learn most easily when their basic needs have been satisfied. Hungry, tired children are less able to think through a situation or consider alternative behavior. In the third example, Crystal's dad may first have given the girls a snack and then cuddled with them to read them a story before helping them figure out how to share the doll carriage. A snack and a story would have satisfied the girls' physical needs for food and a break, and the cuddling their need for affection. These needs would not have been used as motivators for change. Instead, since these needs were satisfied, the girls were free to *figure out how to play together*, meeting both their social needs and those for competency.

Thirteen-year-old Cameron wanted to go to his friend's party to celebrate the beginning of summer vacation. He and his parents had had many discussions about what behaviors or circumstances to avoid at parties: drinking alcoholic beverages, trashing someone's house, sex and/or drugs, accepting dares for unsafe activity. They had a standing agreement that Cameron would call home if anything got out of hand.

Cameron was waiting on his friend's porch when his dad Tony pulled up. He ran to the car.

"Thanks, Dad, for coming to get me," were his first words, as his dad gave him a hug. "There was just too much drinking going on in there, and Nick's parents weren't home like they'd promised."

Tony nodded as he pulled away from the curb.

Tony valued good judgment. He knew people needed information and options in order to exercise good judgment and make good decisions. He had used Cameron's curiosity about his world to give him information about the effects of alcohol and the problems with unsupervised parties. He thought with satisfaction about all the conversations he and Cameron had had. They'd talked about alcohol and its effects on people. They'd talked about the drunk people they'd seen on the streets. More recently, they'd talked about kids' parties and what happened all too often at them. They'd considered ways for Cameron to deal with unsupervised parties, or ones where he might feel uncomfortable. Now Tony felt his son had demonstrated good judgment in calling to be picked up. Tony's approach to keeping his son safe had worked. Cameron recognized the dangers at the party and called his dad.

You can see that some of Cameron's other needs appear to have been satisfied as well. He gave no indication of being hungry or tired. His need for affection was met when his dad gave him a hug. Tony's trust in Cameron, exhibited when Tony let him decide when he was no longer safe, supported Cameron's need to feel good about himself. Tony was reaping the benefits of basing his parenting on his values. He had taught Cameron how to solve problems. He had given his son important, relevant information. Now Cameron knew when he needed to leave the party.

Using Needs to Help Children Learn in a Positive Way

Need	*Encouragement*
Physical	Satisfy with clean water and nourishing food; plenty of rest and exercise.
Protection/Safety	Keep child safe; use car seats, seat belts, and bike helmets; teach about traffic dangers; instruct in the proper use of medicines and household cleaning products.
Social/Affection	Provide loving, ongoing relationships, as well as opportunities to be with other people of all ages.
Curiosity/ Competence	Explain why you want to see certain behavior (your values) and teach child the skills he needs to be able to carry out the values. Encourage child to act in a manner appropriate to his age that demonstrates the value, such as a three-year-old helping out as he is able, with increasing responsibility and skill as he gets older.
Self	Support child's developing sense of self as a person of value and competency. Recognize his abilities and accomplishments with words and deeds.
Aesthetic/Spiritual	Visit places of beauty and cultural meaning; create and enjoy beauty through art, dance, music, craft; attend religious services; practice traditions of importance to you.

Using Needs to Reinforce Children's Learning in a Negative Way

Need	Abuse
Physical	Refuse to feed child or to provide rest or shelter or clothing; excessive use of food and candy as bribes.
Protection/ Safety	Physical punishment: slapping, hitting,spanking; physical abuse: throwing, yanking, pinching, burning, or worse; tying child up; locking child in or out of house; leaving child alone or unsupervised before able to take care of self.
Social/ Affection	Isolate from other people; refuse to care for or support; keep friends away; refuse to touch or hold; ignore; give excessive time-outs; lock in room; speak or look harshly at child most of the time.
Curiosity/ Competence	Punish child for being curious and asking questions, for experimenting with things in the environment; ignore child's need to know; expect child to know something she does not; expect her to do what she cannot; explain nothing; refuse to allow child to do what she can do.
Self	Make fun of child; belittle efforts and accomplishments; use sarcasm or put-downs; laugh at, tease, blame, accuse; destroy gifts from child; refuse affection from child.
Aesthetic/ Spiritual	Refuse to acknowledge or to teach child about the beauty in the world, in all its forms; threaten with God's punishment and hell and damnation.

Parents sometimes use needs as motivators in ways that undermine a child's well-being. For example, they may put the child in an unsafe situation that makes the child fearful and less able to learn. Such methods may also give the child mixed messages. The parent might, for example, be saying, "Don't hit!" while spanking the child, or "Don't yell at me!" while yelling at the child. The chart on page 64 lists some of the negative ways needs are used to motivate children.

As you consider how to react to your child when he or she behaves in a way you do not like, take a few moments to reflect before you act. Taking a few deep breaths at that point can give you the few seconds or minutes it takes to make sure you are about to respond in a way that reflects what you want your child to learn in the long term. Think of your choices that reflect your values.

Reflect, also, on how you can use your child's needs to motivate him or her to live by your values. A child's curiosity and desire to be competent can be powerful motivators when you are teaching values. You have to explain to a child *why* doing something is a good idea, as Cameron's dad did. You have to include children in *planning*, as Nina and Tad did in deciding how to handle family chores. Record on each of your "Analyzing a Value" worksheets (page 167 and your copies) how people's needs can influence the different ways in which you will integrate those values into your family life.

In chapter four you learned the process "Parenting with Values in Mind" (see pages 49–51). Take up a problem you face now in your family and go through this process to help you decide what to do.

Parenting with Values in Mind

Step One: Plan

Describe a situation in your family that needs attention.

Brainstorm—think of as many ideas to deal with the situation as you can.

Make a plan of how to deal with the situation, using your ideas that support your values.

Guide your choice by answering the following questions:
• Which of your values are involved in this situation?
• Which ideas will support the values you just named?
• How will your children's basic needs determine which
  ideas you will include in your plan?

Step Two: Carry out your plan

Whether or not you are ready to put your plan into action right now may depend on other considerations, such as your children's developmental levels, temperament patterns, and learning styles. We will take up these three issues in the chapters that follow.

Step Three: Reflect on your plan

Review your plan. What worked well? What would you do differently another time?

Describe how your children demonstrated that they learned or started to learn what you were trying to teach.

Reflecting on Family Life

Think about something your child did recently.
• What did you do or say to try to motivate your child to change his or her behavior?
• How did he or she respond?
• Did he or she have needs that needed to be satisfied?
• Did he or she have a part in the solution to the problem?
• Would you do the same thing again or try something different?

6

Readiness
to Learn Values

Lillian and her husband wanted to go out to dinner. Lillian telephoned her next door neighbor, Aisha, to see if it was all right to ask her son Charlie to babysit two-month-old Laurie that evening over at his house.

Charlie was only twelve. He was wonderful with Laurie and loved to care for her. He seemed to know exactly what to do to make her happy. He liked having the responsibility of taking care of her. However, the two mothers agreed that he was too young to have complete responsibility for such a little baby. Therefore, Lillian never asked Charlie without first being sure that his mother would be home in case he needed help.

Aisha assured Lillian that she was going to be home, and it was okay for her to ask Charlie to babysit. Aisha hung up the phone, smiling. She felt pleased Charlie was able to be so caring. Her friends felt she was lucky to have such a considerate, thoughtful child. She was not so sure it was luck. She thought of all the times she had helped Charlie understand his sister Zoey, who was just three years younger than he. She remembered when Zoey was born showing Charlie how he could hold her (sitting in a chair with his arm resting on a pillow and being very careful of her wobbly head). She remembered when Charlie would come in from playing and want to give Zoey the kind of bear hug his father gave him. Aisha had to explain what kind of hugs babies liked and how to give one. Constantly, she reminded him when Zoey was little, "Watch her face. That will tell you if she likes what you're doing."

As the two got older, she remembered helping Charlie to include Zoey in his play. (He could build the wooden ramps and each could take turns running the cars down. It was more fun to have two racing cars.) He had learned to think of many ways to make the game fun for both of them.

That relationship still required Aisha's attention. Charlie could not always understand why Zoey did not play as his friends did. As she had

gotten older, Zoey had wanted to have more of a say in how they would play the game. They had argued more. Still, Charlie had the skill of observing another person and of adapting his behaviors to meet the needs of that person. So now he was good at caring for baby Laurie.

Step by step, as they are able developmentally, children learn the information they need and master the complex skills required to be able to live by some values *if they are given guidance.* Caring, as discussed earlier (pages 16–18), is such a value. As illustrated above, building on his interest in his baby sister, Aisha had adapted to Charlie's developmental level as she taught her son to care. At Zoey's birth she had talked about the baby's wobbly head, giving him information, and shown him how to hold her, teaching him skills. Later she had helped Charlie see Zoey's interests in his cars (information) and how they both could race them (skills). As Aisha's reflections illustrate, over an extended period Charlie had continued learning bits of the relevant information and skills needed to be able to care about and for another person. Her encouragement of her children's relationship had kept them involved with each other positively.

At age 12 Charlie still was not ready to assume complete responsibility for someone else. A two-month-old was too vulnerable. He often was not interested in understanding how his own sister was feeling. To stand in the shoes of someone only three years younger (and a sibling, at that) required complex thinking skills and self-control not usually attained by age 12. Charlie still needed guidance from his parents in being able to care.

If you want a child as an adult to have a value that requires knowledge and skills, you must teach both. Your effectiveness as a teacher will increase as you match the knowledge and skills to the child's developmental level.

DEVELOPMENTAL STAGES

From birth to adulthood children pass through an identifiable series of changes in their physical, social, emotional, and thinking behavior. These changes fall into patterns called stages or developmental levels. Change occurs as a result of the child's physiological growth and experiences with people and objects. Understanding children's development will help you as you integrate your values into your parenting.

You can tell a child's level of development by watching and listening. Tracing the physical development of a child is the easiest because it is the most obvious. A baby learns to sit up, then crawl, walk, run and, thus, through stages becomes physically adept. Social development is also fairly easy to observe. Babies move from smiling at others, to reaching out to be picked up, to crying if favorite people leave the room, to eventually having good friends and a close companion.

Following the development of children's emotional life and thinking ability often requires a more conscious and intense effort. For example, a three-year-old excitedly tells Grandma how he will play cars with his new baby brother when the baby comes home from the hospital. He is revealing his enthusiasm for having a new playmate. He is also demonstrating that he literally knows nothing about new babies. He expects the baby to be just like himself. He is also revealing his basic assumption that all the world thinks the same way and wants the same things he does.

Two teenagers, deep in their first love affair, sing songs of parting with little show of emotion. They, too, are revealing their lack of experience, in this instance in having to say the good-byes. They will know differently come the end of summer when he must head to Alaska and she to Virginia. Both styles of thinking, the three-year-old's assuming everyone's thoughts and desires are the same as his and the teenagers' limited experience, impact how effectively children of either age can implement values such as caring and making thoughtful decisions.

LEVELS OF UNDERSTANDING

As you watch and listen to your child, you will know something of how your child feels about and understands a situation. For example, when parents arrive at the child care home, they feel happy at their child's welcome, understanding that his exuberance shows his attachment to them. For the child, the parents' leaving in the morning and returning in the evening help him to understand the comings and goings of life. His joy at seeing his parents and his increasing understanding of life's routines are important parts of a child's development. Knowledge gained by watching and listening to your child helps you know when your child is ready to take the next step in understanding and learning the skills needed to live according to a particular value.

Unfortunately, a parent cannot always tell, even with very careful observation, a child's *level of understanding*. Listening, for instance, to the three- or four-year-old child can frequently mislead you into believing his understanding is much more profound than it is. A child this age can competently use the word "because" and give you a reason for something: "I fell because my sister pushed me," angrily screams the little boy. It is only on reflection that you discover the reason makes no sense, although the statement is grammatically correct. The problem here is that the sister was at school at the time the three-year-old fell! This little boy understands that if his sister pushes him, he is likely to fall—he has experienced that. However, he does not understand the abstract concept that pushing *causes* falling.

Children do not understand the concepts involved or have the ability to manipulate ideas abstractly the way adults can. Grade school children's thinking is different from the three-year-old's and the teenager's. Six-year-old Ellen announced to her mother that she hated all boys and never wanted to play with any of them anymore. When her mother asked about the neighborhood child with whom Ellen played regularly, she assured her mother that "Sam is a friend." Boys and friends were two separate, distinct categories that cannot overlap. Adults, able to deal with ideas abstractly, mentally, can overlap categories and accept one child as both a boy and a friend and another child as a boy and not a friend. Adults think differently from babies, toddlers, and even grade school children. Only with the arrival of the teen years does a person start to be able to think totally abstractly, a characteristic expected of adult thinking.

Even though adults and children think differently, they are both looking intently for answers to life's questions. Both search continuously to make sense out of the world in which they live and seek persistently to find their place in that world. Toddlers try to figure out how the block fits into the box; adults seek to understand why their children grow and develop as they do. Children try to have fun with other children; adults often seek in exasperation to relate to their teenagers who want to be both independent and dependent.

When a person's assumption about something does not "fit" anymore, he will try to figure out why. A four-year-old cannot understand why Dad does not want the baseball he so desperately longs for. He cannot yet grasp his father's perspective. At some point, he sees that Dad does not play with baseballs but instead goes off to play a game of tennis. When one's understanding does not fit one's observations, the child, as he grows, is forced into the next stage of thinking and a greater ability to take the perspective of another person. He perceives that Dad would rather have tennis balls than baseballs ("Dad has different likes than I.").

Parents likewise have to change when something does not fit. For example, parents who have accepted a plan to encourage their son to be more responsible for his homework may start to reconsider when they observe the distress their child is under. They may take another look at the situation and decide there may be other reasons than laziness for the child's behavior. With both the child and the adult, change occurs when experiences do not match assumptions and each is compelled to ask why. This effort to make sense of the world is the common ground between adults and their children.

DEVELOPMENT OF THINKING

An overview of the development of thinking will deepen your understanding obtained through observations of your child. As we have been discussing, observing the development of *both* thinking and emotions is important. The English language, however, makes it difficult to talk about both at the same time. We have words for emotions and words for thinking, but we have no words that tie the two together. As you could see in the preceding examples, though, development of emotions and development of thinking are two sides of the same coin—they cannot be separated.

Our discussion uses the language of thinking, rather than emotions, because it is more precise in helping parents see how their child understands a situation. Remember that your child's emotional development is an intrinsic part of the process. Your two questions will always be, "How does my child understand this situation?" and "How does he or she feel about it?"

Here is a short narrative of the development of thinking at the stages you see in use in "Analyzing a Value" illustrations and exercises. This short guide will help you determine your child's readiness to learn values. By referring to it, you will know how and when to give the information and teach the skills a child will need to learn in order to live by a particular value you have chosen. It will also help you understand how a child sees a situation when her behavior does not meet your expectations.

Babies and toddlers seek to understand and find their way by exploring their social and physical world in the only ways they can. They manipulate, look at, listen to, touch, taste, and smell everything possible to discover what their world is made of and how it works. They manipulate everything possible to see what they can do with it. They interact with everyone possible, thus learning how to satisfy their needs. They learn some things go together and some do not; most people and some objects behave in predictable ways; people and objects exist even when they cannot see, hear, or touch them. They find meaning and understanding by *interacting* with the people and things around them. In short, their learning is *physical*. As they move into toddlerhood, they start putting words to it all. "What's 'at?" they ask.

Babies and toddlers learn values by experiencing them. They learn to trust as their needs are routinely met. The baby who stops crying when she sees her mother opening her blouse to nurse her is demonstrating that trust. Even though she is still so hungry, she knows now—she can anticipate—that food is on the way and she does not need to cry any longer.

Small children begin to learn to care by discovering that living things are different from nonliving things. Things that move on their own are much more interesting than things that do not. If one pulls another baby's hair, he will cry; an animal may bite, scratch, or run away, but a teddy bear does nothing. People who smile, hug, and play with you are by far the most fascinating of all. Learning these similarities and differences is a very early step in learning how to care.

Preschoolers continue to try to understand their world and their place in it by exploring. As they play and interact with other people of all sorts and ages, they learn how to have fun with others. They discover that people are both alike and different from one another and that different people like to do different things. They learn that objects can be props in their play (the same blocks can be a farm or a train), and that Uncle Will makes great paper airplanes but cannot play the piano. They learn by experience that there is more than one way to build a castle and that other people's ideas and feelings must be taken into consideration.

Preschoolers put words to everything and constantly ask, "Why?" The words are as real as the thing they represent: thus, if you are called a monster, you *are* a monster; you become the creature or person represented by the Halloween mask. Their grammar is often on a higher level than their understanding of a situation (recall the three-year-old boy who accused his sister of pushing him even though she was at school). In the preschooler's understanding of his world, people, objects, and words interact for reasons that make no logical sense to the adult because the child has no idea of the underlying abstract relationships among them.

Preschoolers learn values by living them. "Mario can drive the truck to the sand pit and Tommy can fill it," "Emma and Ronny can both push the baby carriage while we shop," "Carrots are healthy," and "Don't you feel good after sleeping all night long?" are literal representations of abstract values. If "sharing" is always giving up the toy to a friend, then sharing means "not having the toy." If "sharing" is giving the friend the toy for three minutes and then getting it back, then sharing means "taking turns." Preschoolers often need help managing the complexities of the world and of integrating values. You need to ask them, "What are some ways that you could all play in the doll corner?" And "What will be the consequences if you don't let your friend have a turn?"

Elementary school-age children's exploration becomes increasingly guided by an abstract system of categories and rules. Their thinking goes something like this: Daddy and I are separate people. Daddy wants tennis balls, while I still want baseballs. Sally likes to build castles, while I like to build roads. Daddy, Sally, and I are all categories, with specific information about each filed within the category. Categories have firm boundaries. Games now have rules, those abstract systems that must be followed with great exactness. Words are now abstractions, representing something but not being the object itself. A child can wear a mask and no longer be in danger of becoming what the mask represents. These children continue to explore their world by physical action, but now they also use words to describe it and abstract concepts to organize it. They no longer have to live everything in order to know it. If their curiosity has not been destroyed, they will soak up information. Their desire to know is limitless.

For elementary school-age children values now become a system for organizing information and guiding behavior. They want to know about drugs, and classify them into "good" drugs for medicinal purposes or "bad" drugs that are illegal, no questions asked. Staying healthy means taking the medicinal drug and following the doctor's prescription exactly. These children want to know about people they see who wear glasses or have hearing aids or use canes. For them, caring is remembering to hold the photograph to the light or speak louder or walk more slowly.

From ages six to twelve, a child can think of many ways to deal with a situation, but may have difficulty thinking through all of the issues raised by an emergency. She has difficulty understanding how categories can overlap. For example, a particular boy can be a friend though she hates most boys. She simply does not think of her friend as a "boy." Likewise, believing in the dangers of illegal drugs, a child this age would not be able to consider that illegal drugs might have medicinal value, or that rules can be broken if everyone agrees to it. Thus, Charlie was a wonderful babysitter for two-month-old Laurie as long as all went according to routine. His mother had to be available in case of emergency.

Teenagers finally start to have the ability to think abstractly. Thought no longer needs to be tied to object. Categories can overlap: a friend can be a person who is also a member of the "hated boys" category. Teens can now see new relationships and interrelationships. This ability makes them question everything. "Why is it okay to take aspirin, but not smoke marijuana? Both relieve pain." The stranger one talks to on the bus is not a total stranger, but still not the close friend of many years. Teenagers search for their identity: who are they now and who do they want to become? They can see more possibilities, as well as the pros and cons of each. Today, their answer might be to become a doctor, and they are into the medical aspects of someone's health. Next week, the plan may be to become an actor, and life is lived with dramatic speech and exaggerated action.

Part of the teenager's search is to question, with increasing insight and wonder, the values by which he or she has been raised. "You say you care, but you're doing nothing about _____." Or "Living a healthy lifestyle means not eating red meat. What are you doing?" Or "I don't care about _____. They had the same chance at an education that we all did."

Development of Thinking

Stage	Level of thinking
Baby/ Toddler	Deals with physical world; shows by behavior that she organizes and categorizes life around her by what goes together and what does not.
	Learns to anticipate; learns what is out of sight still exists.
	Asks, "What's 'at?"
Toddler/ Preschool	Learns to put words to all he is doing and exploring.
	He thinks everyone feels and thinks as he does.
	The real and the pretend worlds are not clearly differentiated.
	Asks, "Why?"
School age	Organizes world according to abstract, discrete principles.
	Sees that people have different needs than herself.
	Her pretend world is now distinct from the real world.
	She follows rules exactly. Sees issues and people as either all "right" or "wrong" or "good" or "bad."
Teenage	Can manipulate ideas abstractly. Categories can overlap.
	Rules can be broken if all agree, fairness being the abstract concept that overrides rules.
	A person can be a mix of "good" and "bad" qualities.
	Questions everything.

Children's thinking is different from adults'. It is important to remember this fact, especially when your children have advanced verbal skills. Even when they become teenagers and look more like adults in size and form, their thinking is still different from adults' because they have much less experience with life.

In addition to cognitive development, remember to consider how the other three aspects of your child's growth–physical, emotional, and social–affect being able to live by your values. Write on your "Analyzing a Value" worksheets under "Teaching or preserving the value" (pages 166-167 and your copies) the developmental steps that your child needs to master to be able to live by each of your values.

In the exercise below, expand your thinking to include what your child needs to learn and is ready to learn.

Parenting with Values in Mind

Step One: Plan

Describe a situation in your family that needs attention.

Brainstorm—think of as many ideas to deal with the situation as you can.

Make a plan of how to deal with the situation, using your ideas that support your values.

Guide your choice by answering the following questions:
• Which of your values are involved in this situation?
• Which ideas will support the values you just named?
• How will your children's basic needs determine which ideas you will include in your plan?

• How will your children's developmental levels affect which ideas you decide to put into action?

Step Two: Carry out your plan

Whether or not you are ready to put your plan into action right now may depend on other considerations, such as your children's temperament patterns and learning styles. We will discuss these two issues in the next two chapters.

Step Three: Reflect on your plan

Review your plan. What worked well? What would you do differently another time?

Describe how your children demonstrated that they learned or started to learn what you were trying to teach.

Reflecting on Family Life

As you observe the developmental steps children pass through in gaining understanding and meaning in their lives,
• Did you identify the kind of thinking your child does now?
• How should your child's thinking style influence your ways of living with and guiding him or her?
• Does your child seem to be able to meet the expectations you set?
• Are the expectations you set challenging your child?

7

Considering Temperament Patterns

That weekend Maria had taken her two children, Josh, 5, and Alexis, 3, to Belinda's birthday party. With no hesitation, Josh had walked in, joined a group, and become involved in a game. Alexis would not leave her mom even when Belinda's mother Sara, whom she knew well, tried to coax her. Only when the girls started decorating paper bags did Alexis finally leave her mother's side.

Maria, talking about the party with Sara, sighed, "I want Alexis to be assertive. She will need to be with the way the work world is out there. I don't have to worry about Josh. He already is assertive, but Alexis just draws back."

"You may be able to teach her some coping skills as she gets older," suggested Sara.

"Like what?"

"Well, she finally joined the group when we started decorating the bags. She likes that work. Maybe you could arrive when an activity she likes is getting started. Then when she sees she can have a good time she won't hang back so much. Maybe going with a friend or her dad would help—she may have a harder time leaving you. Or maybe arriving early before the crowd shows up would help. That's what I do when I'm going to one of those business parties I hate," Sara laughed. "You know I have the same problem as Alexis. That's why I can come up with so many ideas. And I always remind myself about the good times and try to forget the ones that aren't."

"What you're saying is that at this stage of her development I need to help her find ways of coping with her pattern of pulling back. Maybe later when she's older she can think of ways herself," said Maria.

What is a
temperament pattern?

A temperament pattern is a consistent way in which people respond to their world. In determining a pattern, you must be able to observe it under many conditions. To identify a pattern in activity level, for example, observe your child over a period of time as he sleeps, eats, plays, listens to a story, and watches television. Does he move a lot or a little?

Patterns can be identified from early infancy on. Josh and Alexis's contrasting behavior is related to their pattern of approaching people or objects. As their mother confirmed, their behavior at the party was typical for them.

Mothers have always known that babies have individual, identifiable patterns as to how they respond to the world. Janey was active even while in the womb. It seemed to her mother she was always kicking and squirming around. Tyler was very predictable. From early infancy he went to sleep and woke up at the same times. He also cried from hunger within fifteen minutes of the same time everyday. Babies have their patterns.

Ten Temperament
Traits

Read each trait's description. The line below it represents a range from one extreme to the other for that trait. Estimate your child's temperament pattern by deciding whether her behavior falls at one of the extremes or somewhere in the middle. Consider her behavior in many different situations. Compare her behavior to that of other children. Mark the line.

Activity

A child's overall preference for active or inactive play; a child's overall energy level throughout the day. *Best clue:* Leaving television and video games aside, what things would your child do if left to his own devices? Would he be "on the go" or idle?

Low activity	High activity
Calm and slow moving	Wild and quick moving

└────┴────┴────┴────┴────┴────┘

Adaptability

How easily a child adjusts to attempts to influence what she is doing or thinking. *Best clue:* Does your child adapt quickly to changes, new places, ideas, expectations? Is it difficult or easy for your child when there is a new routine or schedule?

Fast adapting   Slow adapting
Easygoing   Strong willed

└──────┴──────┴──────┴──────┴──────┴──────┘

Approach

A child's initial tendency for responding to a new experience, a new person, or a new environment. *Best clue:* What is your child's first and usual reaction to new people, situations, or places?

Quick approach   Slow approach
Outgoing/Eager   Slow to warm/Withdrawing

└──────┴──────┴──────┴──────┴──────┴──────┘

Distractibility

How easily things going on around him interrupt a child's thought processes or attention. *Best clue:* Is your child very aware and easily diverted by noises and people? Does he get sidetracked from what you said when something else catches his attention? Can you distract him from upset feelings by redirecting his attention?

Low distractibility   High distractibility
Not easily diverted   Easily diverted

└──────┴──────┴──────┴──────┴──────┴──────┘

Emotional sensitivity

The ease or difficulty with which a child responds emotionally to a situation. This trait has two sub-scales, one for sensitivity to one's own feelings and one for sensitivity to others' feelings. *Best clue:* Does your child often become upset "over nothing" or does she rarely become upset even when circumstances suggest that she could? Does the child feel sympathy for or empathy with others?

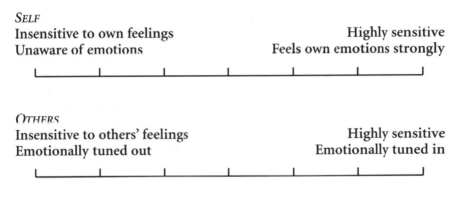

Self

| Insensitive to own feelings | Highly sensitive |
| Unaware of emotions | Feels own emotions strongly |

Others

| Insensitive to others' feelings | Highly sensitive |
| Emotionally tuned out | Emotionally tuned in |

Intensity

The amount of energy a child commonly uses to express emotions. *Best clue:* How physically dramatic, fierce, or passionate is your child when expressing strong feelings? Is he easy or hard to "read?"

| Low intensity | High intensity |
| Mild reactions | Dramatic reactions |

Mood

The amount of pleasant, joyful, and friendly behavior as contrasted with unpleasant, crying, and unfriendly behavior. *Best clue:* Does your child tend to view the world as primarily a positive or primarily a negative place? Is she an optimist or a pessimist? Lighthearted or serious?

| Positive mood | Negative mood |
| Happy-go-lucky/Optimistic | Somber/Pessimistic |

Persistence

The length of time a child will continue to make an effort, especially when the task gets hard. *Best clue:* Does he stick with things even when frustrated? Can he stop an activity when asked to?

High persistence   Low persistence
Gets "locked in"   Stops easily

L_____|_____|_____|_____|_____|_____|_____J

Regularity

The day-to-day predictability of hunger, sleep, and elimination. Consider each function separately and rate it on its own scale. *Best clue:* Does your child normally tend to go to bed, wake up, or have bowel movements at the same time each day?

HUNGER
Wants food at same time   Irregular eater

L_____|_____|_____|_____|_____|_____J

SLEEP
Tired on schedule   No schedule

L_____|_____|_____|_____|_____|_____J

ELIMINATION
BM's at same time daily   Try and guess

L_____|_____|_____|_____|_____|_____J

Sensory awareness

How sensitive a child is in each of her sensory channels: 1) pain, 2) touch, 3) taste, 4) smell, 5) hearing, and 6) sight. Rate each channel on a separate scale. *Best clue:* How aware of noises, temperature changes, lights, odors, flavors, and textures is your child? How does she respond to pain? It is possible for a child to be very aware in some channels and unaware in others.

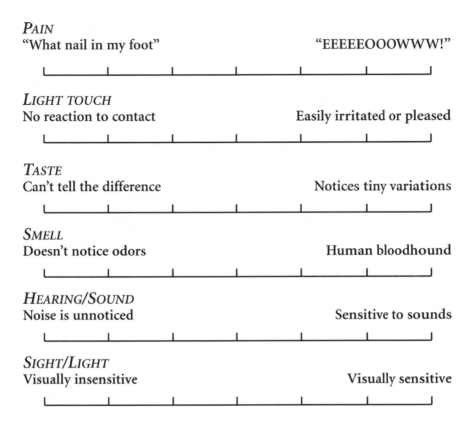

PAIN
"What nail in my foot"   "EEEEEOOOWWW!"

LIGHT TOUCH
No reaction to contact   Easily irritated or pleased

TASTE
Can't tell the difference   Notices tiny variations

SMELL
Doesn't notice odors   Human bloodhound

HEARING/SOUND
Noise is unnoticed   Sensitive to sounds

SIGHT/LIGHT
Visually insensitive   Visually sensitive

(Temperament trait descriptions and scale reprinted from *Understanding Temperament: Strategies for Creating Family Harmony* by Lyndall Shick, M.A. Used with permission from Parenting Press, Inc.)

Interestingly, certain physiological responses seem to go along with certain temperament patterns. Young children who tend to be inhibited, to withdraw from social gatherings, for instance, also tend to have a faster heart rate and higher right brain activity than do children who enter into a group more easily. This kind of relationship between behavior and physiology seems to imply that behavior is biologically determined and, therefore, cannot be changed. For parents this raises the question of how to deal with a temperament pattern, especially if the pattern interferes with a child's healthy growth.

TEMPERAMENT PATTERNS
AND VALUES

Researchers and parents have found that parents and their children can learn to cope with temperament patterns. Children can be helped to learn how to deal with their feelings and the situations that produce them. Maria was taking this approach as she thought through how to help her daughter be more assertive. If patterns can be coped with, the challenge for you is to figure out how best to help your child deal with temperament patterns that hinder his or her development. *Understanding Temperament: Strategies for Creating Family Harmony* by Lyndall Shick gives many useful suggestions for how parents can build on the strengths of their children's temperaments and help their children cope with weaknesses. (See page 173 for reference.)

A child's temperament pattern may make it easier for her to acquire her parent's values. For instance, let us say that you want your child to be *involved*. An involved person would be able to take up a project with interest and enthusiasm and stay with it until it is completed. This is a description of the temperament pattern *persistent*. Thus, being persistent would support the value of involvement. From infancy Carmen was persistent. She would take a toy and explore it by shaking it, mouthing it, trying to make it slide or wave. Carmen was involved with the toy longer and did more things with it than would most babies. She was persistent. Because of this trait, her temperament helped her become an involved person.

Values also can provide a means for you to analyze the impact of temperament patterns on your developing child. Maria's view that *assertiveness* is important for a person in today's world alerted her to the disadvantages of her daughter's tendency to draw back in social situations. The value gave Maria a means of assessing the impact of Alexis's temperament pattern on her development.

Temperament patterns can often stand in the way of children acquiring desired behaviors. Zachary was very distractible. His parents wanted him to be responsible. One part of being *responsible*, they felt, was to take care of one's possessions. Zachary, in his distractible way, would let his possessions fall where they might when something else caught his attention. He would drop his bike in the middle of the driveway when his neighborhood friends called to him to join them in a game of baseball. He left his glove on the field when the gang went over to one child's house for water. His temperament pattern worked to the disadvantage of his ability to acquire his parents' value.

Temperament patterns can be supportive of some values while under mining others. The persistent child stays with an activity, tends to become *involved* easily, her parents' value. She can also have great difficulty moving from one activity to another. She wants to finish the task even though it is bedtime, dinnertime, or time to leave a friend's house. Such children are not adaptable or flexible, which also may be their parents' values.

The challenge for you when temperament patterns hinder your child's development of a value you hold is to find ways to help your child cope. Maria was doing this as she thought through how she could help Alexis deal with new situations. Zachary's parents, recognizing his distractibility, will acknowledge that he needs more time to become responsible than a child who is less distractible. Early on, they might encourage him to think about where he might have left his toy, rather than tell him where it is: "Your ball glove is not in the closet. Where did you leave it?" Or "When did you have it last? Can you remember what you did next after the last time you used it?" They would not say, "Pick up the ball glove you left in the driveway." Their focus would be to help Zachary remember what he did with his glove, to help him be able to retrace his steps. Once he could do this, their comment might be shortened to "I don't see the glove in the closet." The value of responsibility guides the parents' process of teaching their child how to be responsible. Zachary's parents, knowing his temperament pattern of distractibility, are willing to give him more time and direction, but they are not willing to give up their value.

Awareness of how values and temperament patterns may be interacting will make your expectations more realistic and your teaching of values more effective. Record these relationships for each of your values on your "Analyzing a Value" worksheets (page 167 and your copies).

Here is a chance for you to include temperament considerations in your thinking about how to deal with a situation in your family. Practice using the "Parenting with Values in Mind" process again in the exercise below and this time incorporate the knowledge you gained from doing the temperament analysis of your child or children.

Parenting with Values in Mind

Step One: Plan

Describe a situation in your family that needs attention.

Brainstorm—think of as many ideas to deal with the situation as you can.

Make a plan of how to deal with the situation, using your ideas that support your values.

Guide your choice by answering the following questions:

• Which of your values are involved in this situation?

• Which ideas will support the values you just named?

• How will your children's basic needs determine which ideas you will include in your plan?

• How will your children's developmental levels affect which ideas you decide to put into action?

• How will your children's temperament patterns affect which ideas you decide to put into action and how you will do so?

Step Two: Carry out your plan

Whether or not you are ready to put your plan into action right now may depend on one other consideration, your child's learning style. We will discuss this issue in the next chapter.

Step Three: Reflect on your plan

Review your plan. What worked well? What would you do differently another time?

Describe how your children demonstrated that they learned or started to learn what you were trying to teach.

Reflecting on Family Life

- Identify your own temperament, using the same scale as you used earlier to identify your child's temperament.
- Think about how your child's temperament affected the outcome of a recent situation you faced.
- How did your own temperament affect it?

8

Working with Learning Styles

Naomi, her stomach churning, watched her thirteen-year-old son Grant wander around their apartment when he was supposed to be doing his homework. She, her husband Matt, and the school personnel had agreed that Grant was old enough to assume responsibility for his homework. If he didn't get it done, the teachers would deal with it. His parents were not to intervene. Naomi and Matt had felt comfortable with the plan. They wanted their child to be responsible. Now Naomi had doubts about the plan and their assumptions.

All through elementary school Grant had been a good student. He had liked school, done his homework, and achieved well. The problems had started with seventh grade. The quality of his work had slipped. His reports became more skimpy when he should have been expanding topics. Only in math and science had he maintained his grades and his interest.

As Naomi watched, Grant went from his desk to the refrigerator for a snack, back to his desk, then to the bathroom and back to his desk, then off to get a drink. He never really settled down to the social studies assignment. This behavior was not like her son of just two years ago. In sixth grade he had built elaborate social studies projects. One that she remembered was a volcano made out of papier-mache. He'd used baking soda and vinegar to have it spout like an erupting volcano. But those assignments had been projects with a minimum of reading or writing. Now assignments involved writing a paper using several sources to get information.

"You know," Naomi said, discussing the issue with Matt, "I don't think it's just his lack of responsibility that's going on with Grant's homework. After his hour of snacking and playing outside he came in and completed his math assignment. Then he started this restless wandering around. By then, he could be tired or hungry. It was just before supper. But the behav-

ior continued after supper. He just did not settle down, and I know the assignment is due tomorrow. I'm not sure he has even started it.

"I know I'm not supposed to interfere. I can't, however, keep from asking myself why the change in him? Yes, he's into adolescence. But the work is different, too. In fifth and sixth grades his social studies assignments were all those projects for which he had to write a summary. Now the assignments are reading and answering rather complicated questions. I looked at his social studies book after he went to bed. The writing isn't simple. The questions take thinking. They aren't just finding the answer and copying it out of a book.

"I'm beginning to wonder if something else is going on with Grant. Maybe his behavior isn't just a lack of being responsible. Maybe he needs help. Are his academic skills adequate for what's expected of him? I wonder if other children are having similar problems?"

Naomi, observing her child closely, had questions about the expectations they had for Grant. Maybe their expecting Grant to be responsible for his school work was exaggerating a problem rather than helping him learn responsibility. Her concerns were supported by several observations. She noted his amazing change in attitude towards school, especially related to social studies. She was very aware of the differences in the kind of work expected of Grant in sixth and eighth grades. The teachers expected the students to read for meaning and not to have to review the material in class. Major assignments were papers, not projects. The value of wanting their son to assume responsibility was valid. The question she and Matt had to answer was whether or not he was able to assume total responsibility for his school work.

For many children their learning style makes it difficult for them to meet ordinary expectations. These children are often very bright. It is easy to judge them as lazy and irresponsible. Rather than labeling him, however, Grant's mother reviewed his history and observed his behavior.

Naomi started asking questions about the expectations she, her husband, and the educational team had put on Grant. Were there reasons for his inability to meet their expectation of personal responsibility?

WHAT IS A LEARNING STYLE?

Learning is the process of taking in information, remembering it, and being able to use it appropriately. Learning style, as used in this book, does not include how a person thinks, that is, how a person manipulates ideas. Learning style is a person's strongly preferred mode of taking in and/or remembering information. Visual learners are people who rely heavily on their eyes and visual imagery to take in information. Auditory learners are listeners. They can follow verbal instructions. Others seem to learn through movement. They learn best if they can learn by doing. Most people learn effectively using any and all of the ways of taking in information. (There are many terms for different learning styles. Learning disabilities, dyslexia, minimal brain function, etc. refer to problems that can interfere with a person's learning and are not discussed in this book.)

PROBLEMS RELATED TO LEARNING STYLE

In a perfect world, learning style would seldom be a problem because instruction would take advantage of all modes of learning. Parents and teachers would demonstrate as they talk. Unfortunately, many schools do not teach in all learning modes. Some school problems develop when the strengths of a child's style do not match the teaching style. Frequently, when children start to learn to read the issue becomes obvious for the first time. The teacher may emphasize a visual mode, the "look-say" method of sight reading, which is apt to cause problems for the weak visual learner. The reverse can also happen. Relying on an auditory teaching method (phonics) is apt to produce problems for the weak auditory learner.

Problems can develop as the child moves through school, as ways of presenting material change. A child whose learning style was supported in one grade may be left struggling in another. Grant is an example. He could get the content that was reviewed in class. He could do the assignments that included projects and minimal writing. Longer papers were difficult. Many students have difficulty with the eye-hand coordination required when hand writing. (A computer may be the solution for many of these students.) Unless an alert adult picks up on the situation, the child is likely to perform miserably and acquire negative labels as he or she moves through school.

VALUES AND
LEARNING STYLES

Learning styles are important in the acquisition of values in two ways. One is that your expectations may need to be adjusted. Even though his parents continue to want him to be responsible, Grant needs help. He may even need testing to identify his learning style and, consequently, how he can best be helped. Children can learn to compensate for their learning style. Usually this is more efficiently accomplished if the child has some help. Teachers also often will adapt their methods, as they come to understand the child's problem. However, to expect the child to be responsible and to function independently and well is unreasonable if he has a learning style that makes learning under certain conditions difficult.

Second, knowing a child has an extreme preference in her learning style can alert you to use that mode when communicating with her. For a visual learner, being given a written list of chores that she can see is easier to manage than being told. An auditory learner can benefit by listening, as often as she wishes, to her chores on a tape recorder. This has the advantage of seeming less like nagging, too. For the kinesthetic learner, you can work with her for a few minutes to get her started on the task and explain what is expected and then leave her to continue on her own. Each way of letting the child know what you want honors the child's learning style and gives her a chance to succeed in being responsible. Note that you still hold the value. How the child moves towards living by it is adapted. Expectations are not changed. The time table for acquiring the value and maybe even the method of setting it are changed. Record how learning styles might affect how you teach or integrate each of your values into family life on your "Analyzing a Value" worksheets (page 167 and your copies).

Incorporate knowledge of your child's learning style into your consideration below of a situation you want to resolve. Remember that the more you practice the process of "Parenting with Values in Mind," the more adept you will become at using it and the more helpful it will be.

Parenting with Values in Mind

Step One: Plan

Describe a situation in your family that needs attention.

Brainstorm—think of as many ideas to deal with the situation as you can.

Make a plan of how to deal with the situation, using your ideas that support your values.

Guide your choice by answering the following questions:
• Which of your values are involved in this situation?
• Which ideas will support the values you just named?
• How will your children's basic needs determine which ideas you will include in your plan?
• How will your children's developmental levels affect which ideas you decide to put into action?
• How will your children's temperament patterns affect which ideas you decide to put into action?
• How will your children's learning styles affect which ideas you decide to put into action?

Step Two: Carry out your plan

Now is the time to put your plan into action. You have considered all aspects of the situation and your child that are required for you to act according to your values successfully.

Step Three: Reflect on your plan

Review your plan. What worked well? What would you do differently another time?

Describe how your children demonstrated that they learned or started to learn what you were trying to teach.

Reflecting on Family Life

- What learning style have you observed in your child?
- What are his actions and successes and failures that enable you to iden-tify his learning style?
- What recent challenge would have been easier to deal with if you had taken into consideration his learning style?

9

Resolving Conflicting Values

Values have an impact on each other. They can build and strengthen each other or they can pull in opposite directions, undermining the effectiveness of each one. Parents need to consider all their values as a whole. In the example below another of the mothers in the parenting discussion group acknowledges inconsistencies in her values.

"You know my eleven-year-old daughter Megan and I have a good time together. I want that relationship to continue. We plan something special together every week, maybe just fifteen minutes but usually closer to an hour. We always seem to have a lot to talk about.

"Well, one of my values is that we spend money wisely. Megan has an allowance. We thought this would be a good way for her to learn how to manage her money. It hasn't worked. She's always broke, always having to ask for money. There are always things she feels she just has to have. Yet within a month the stuff will be lying around unused.

"This week I started thinking about what we like to do together. It's go out and shop. We wander around the mall, talking and looking at clothes. I inevitably buy something I don't really need and she does, too. Talk about conflicting messages!

"So this week I talked to her about our shopping trips. She said maybe we could sew instead. We both enjoy that. We can talk at the same time, and she has a skirt she's needed help with for over two months.

"What this made me realize is how easy it is to give our children conflicting messages. I was living by one of my values, keeping my relationships going. Implementing that value by shopping was undermining another value. It's complicated to parent with values in mind!"

෨൸

Karen recognized that she was giving Megan conflicting messages. Their spontaneous shopping expeditions were not supporting her value of helping Megan spend her money carefully. Think back to Lynne, in chapter four, who wanted her children to be aware of what was going on in their world, but not of the sadness of their grandfather dying.

The question these kinds of situations raise is, am I giving clear, consistent messages about my values in what I say and what I do, or are my values in conflict?

Values can build and strengthen each other, too, as this story from Romano's mother shows:

෨൸

Seven-year-old Romano has invited a new friend over for the afternoon. He wants it to be fun for both of them. "I think we'll build with Legos®," he tells his mother. "Jason tells me he has a lot of Legos®. We'll also ride bikes. He's bringing his. Oh, and Mom, can we have toasted cheese sandwiches instead of peanut butter and jelly? He doesn't like peanut butter. Can you imagine anyone not liking peanut butter?"

෨൸

Romano's parents value caring, self-direction, and clear thinking. Romano is demonstrating each of them. His concern about what his new friend likes demonstrates that he is able to care. His thoughts about what would be fun show that he can think clearly. The fact that he did all the planning shows that he is able to guide himself.

Each of the three values build on, support, and moderate each other. Romano is acting independently. He made his own plan. The fact that he could think clearly about what Jason likes and what they could do together supports his ability to act independently. Both the independence and the thinking, however, would work on Jason's behalf because Romano's caring influenced them. Romano wants both his friend and himself to have a good time. The values support each other.

Values can moderate each other. Self-directed people will be more capable if they can think through issues abstractly than will those who cannot. Thus, the values of clear thinking or having good judgment or being intelligent will support the value of being self-directed. In addition, the caring will moderate the individualism, and even possibly self-centeredness, that can be an outcome of being self-directed.

As you read through this chapter, use the worksheets on pages 168 and 170 within the "Family Guide" to sort out how your values and those of your parenting partner affect each other. First, list your values that support each other and/or help another value to develop on page 168.

VALUES IN CONFLICT

Values, even desirable values, can conflict with each other. Parents want children to be adaptable and yet able to say "no." They want them to be flexible and still persistent, or self-directed, an independent thinker, and yet be cooperative. Is there a way to have it all?

∞

Following the neighborhood potluck, Letitia described to her husband how their son, Antonio, had again made her stop and think about what she was doing. "I want him to be adaptable, but I also want him to be able to say 'No.' Hardly anyone at the potluck was trying the Thai food our new neighbors had brought. So here I am urging Antonio to be caring, to show consideration for this family and try their food, and he is saying 'No.' All at once it hit me how my values were in conflict. I want him to say 'No' to what I want him to say 'No' to, but I don't want him to say 'No' if I think it means he won't be caring."

∞

Conflicts arise between values. A frequent one occurs when parents want their children to be respectful *and* curious. For many of us, being respectful includes not touching other people's property (including the crystal dog on the coffee table). But the curious toddler touches as well as looks at everything. Which value is the toddler to follow, her curiosity or being respectful of another's property? Being respectful may also mean not questioning an adult, a process the clear-thinking teenager needs to practice. Urging children to be respectful and curious, both, can give very confusing messages to them.

Review your list of values again. List on page 168 those values that you see now are in conflict.

YOUR PARTNER'S VALUES

Parenting partners have values, too. What are your partner's values? Just as your own values can support or undermine each other, your partner's values can support and reinforce or undermine and negate yours. *This is one of the biggest potential sources of conflict between parents.*

Have your parenting partner identify her or his values using the ideas and materials presented in chapter two on pages 19–36. List your partner's values on "Identifying My Parenting Partner's Values" on page 165.

Your values and those of your partner can build and strengthen each other. Partners with the same values have a standard on which to build their plans as to how to guide their children. If both of you value creativity, accepting the clutter of clay and paints or the construction of a space ship out of boxes will be less irritating than if you did not share the value. If both of you hope to see your child self-confident, then you will deal with put-downs if they creep into the family conversation. Common values give a basis for deciding how to nurture children. List on page 170 the values you share in common.

Partners' values can also support each other in ways similar to how your own values can support each other. One partner valuing clear thinking and the other caring can support each other's efforts to help their children adopt both values, just as one parent who has chosen both of these values can do. List on page 170 the values that support each other.

Your partner's values can conflict with yours in the same manner that your own values can be in conflict. For example, parents frequently differ as to how to deal with feelings. One parent values being strong. To him, being strong means being able to deal with all situations, including being above feeling sorrow or disappointment. The other partner values being aware of and expressing one's feelings. When the child's dear pet dies one parent will be saying, "This is life. You can't let it get you down. Go out and have a run. It will make you feel better." The other parent will be consoling, "It's sad when a pet dies. You're going to miss him. You two had such fun together." This parent is apt to hold the crying child close. Values can lead to conflicting behavior. List on page 170 your values that are in conflict with your partner's. Describe the conflict.

When parents differ, as in this case, they need to be aware of the consequences of their differences. Do you find yourselves criticizing each other? "You are making him soft." "He is only a child." Is your child receiving mixed messages? "You must not show your feelings." "Feelings are a part of life. It's all right to show them in appropriate ways." Is your child learning several different ways of dealing with problems? Or do the differences go in such diverse directions that the child receives confusing, opposing sets of instructions? Are the differences undermining the child's ability to develop a set of values?

Resolving conflicts over values, whether they be conflicts between one person's values or between those of partners, results in smoother family functioning. You will have a clearer vision of how you want to handle situations. Children will be better able to anticipate what is expected. Messages to them will be clearer. There is less likelihood that your children will be able to manipulate their parents. Parents will have fewer conflicts.

Discussing how to deal with conflicts is easier when they occur between two people, even though the same process seems to go on when you look at your own personal conflicts. Here are three examples of couples dealing with their conflicts.

Ken and Margo are disagreeing on an aspect of discipline with two-year-old Amelia, who does not always do exactly what Mom or Dad wish.

"Children should obey," Ken said adamantly. "When I tell Amelia to stop, she needs to stop! Parking lots and sidewalks by busy streets are just too dangerous. That is why I list obedience as a value. She should stop other times when I tell her to, too. Take today, she just kept looking at me and dumping the beads after I had told her not to. I want an obedient child, not one who is spoiled and completely out of bounds!"

"You're implying that I spoil her," said Margo, as adamant and angry as Ken. "I don't think so. Today she tried to run from me in the parking lot. I grabbed her hand and gave her two choices. She could hold my hand or we could get back in the car. I told her it was too dangerous to run in the parking lot. She wanted to go to the dollar store so she took my hand. If she hadn't wanted to go to the store, I would have told her her choices were to hold my hand or be carried to the store.

"I don't want a child who obeys without thinking," continued Margo. "That makes a compliant child. And that is what you get when you demand obedience. When you sent Amelia to her room it wasn't for dumping the beads, but because she didn't obey you. Do you want a compliant child who does what she's told? I don't want her to follow the first boyfriend who wants to have sex with her. I don't want her to take whatever drug someone offers her. I want her to stop and think, 'Is this what I really want? What will be the consequences if I do this?' That is why I value clear thinking. That is why I want her to think of alternatives and consequences."

"You're being ridiculous," said Ken disdainfully. "Of course I don't want Amelia to have sex with whomever comes along or take whatever drugs are offered to her. She's only 2 years old! I want her to be obedient now when she's perfectly incapable of making those kinds of decisions and doesn't need to. We're always with her."

"But we won't always be. We have to prepare her for that future," said Margo in a defiant manner.

"We also have to keep her safe now. When she runs away from us in a parking lot, she's in real danger," retorted Ken.

"You're right. We agree there. We both want her safe. We come at it differently. I deal with reasons, choices, and consequences. You use ultimatums. Where we differ is in how we keep her safe ten years from now."

"I hadn't thought about what we were doing now as preparing her for later. And she can think of alternatives. The ones she came up with last night when we were thinking of ways of going upstairs were very imaginative," Ken chuckled. "But take the beads . . ."

"My problem with emphasizing obedience is that, when I'm disciplining her, blind obedience may shift the emphasis away from what I want her to learn. Today when she dumped those beads you sent her to her room for disobeying you. I feel she needed to deal with the dumping of the beads. Dumping beads is not the way to take care of toys. Now as I think about it—which I can't usually do at the moment of the problem—I would have given her a choice. I might have said to her, 'If you dump the beads you can help pick them up or we will put them away for a while.' I want her to learn to be responsible for her things. I want her to learn consequences. To be able to think clearly, one has to know there are consequences and to anticipate what they might be. Knowing what will happen when she dumps beads is a beginning step in learning about consequences."

Ken observed, "What you're telling me is that you value obedience as much as I do. It's the method we use to get what we want that differs."

This couple resolved their conflict by listening to each other and finding common ground for understanding. Basically, they held the same value. Both wanted their daughter to be obedient and safe. Their differences lay in their means of implementing their values. Margo had a longer perspective. She saw what she was doing now as preparing Amelia for her teen years. Since Mike's value of obedience was not based on a personal need for power and he saw the importance of helping Amelia start to learn how to make decisions, he was willing to try to adapt his ways of dealing with Amelia to be more compatible with Margo's.

Conflicts cannot always be resolved, as you will see with Jack and Linda, below.

Jack works as an executive in a high stress industry. When he comes home in the evening he hopes to find a refuge from the tense negotiating and fast pace of the office, with its clutter of unfinished business. Linda works part-time and is able to be at home with their children one day a week.

"I just don't know why the kids can't clean up after themselves," ranted Jack as he stormed in the door. "David's coat is on the floor in the entry way with his back pack. Vickie's dolls are all over the living room floor. It would be nice to come home to an orderly house. Kids need to know how to take care of their things. They need to value orderliness."

Linda continued stirring the soup. Having an orderly house was not high on her list of values. Since David had come home from school, she and the two children had been busy making candle holders with pine cones and dried grasses they'd collected by the roadside. She'd lost track of time and all at once had to rush to get dinner on the table. She knew the family room was a mess, too.

The condition of the house was a continuous argument between the couple. Jack liked everything to be in place. Linda liked to be able to find things, but she also liked doing projects, and these were often messy.

Dinner was a rather tense time. When Jack was angry he didn't talk. Linda got angry. She resented his wanting things so neat. She liked her projects and felt it was good the children were getting involved in them, too. Of course, coats and back packs should be put away, but that should not be a big deal.

When the children were settled, Linda confronted Jack: "I'm tired of your always harping about the house. This is my one day home with the kids. We had a wonderful time finding grasses and making candle holders. But being busy makes messes. We ran out of time. At least there was dinner on the table. And you didn't even look at the pretty candle holders the kids made for their grandparents. All you could do was fuss that there were dolls in the living room and David's coat in the entry way!"

"Well, I come home and I've worked hard all day, I'd like a little order."

"The table was set and the dinner was good. Couldn't you focus on that?" Linda asked furiously.

"No! There was too much mess to get to that. At the office there are always people in and out needing this, wanting to talk about that. Putting stuff on my desk. I need some order when I get home."

"And I need to be able to do my projects and get the kids involved in them. It was great to be out this afternoon and find those grasses. I want our children to enjoy nature."

"Oh, come on . . . so do I. . . . But does it have to be all over the house?"

"It's not all over the house. There's nothing in our bedroom."

"Yes, but the bed's not made, and there's no place to sit."

"Well, if we made the bed when we got out of it in the morning, it would be made," countered Linda. "We could take that old chair you say is your favorite but you never sit in and put it by the window. There's room."

"But I'd still have to walk through the clutter to get there. I still think we should be working on the kids to put their things away. Why does David insist on dropping his coat in the entry way?"

"Then you deal with it."

"Why should I?"

"Because it's important to you. I'm after him about so many other things, like doing his homework, I don't want to add more things. He'll learn to hang up his coat when he's ready."

ᘒᓬᕣ

Jack and Linda value neatness very differently. In their argument they were not able to move beyond their own personal needs or lack thereof for orderliness. They had no discussion of the children's needs to learn to be responsible for their things or to learn to put things away so they could be found later. Linda did try to brainstorm options for meeting Jack's needs, but he could not accept any of her suggestions. His value of orderliness was primary. In cases like this where there are such strong differences, parents may be wise to seek counseling.

ᕫᕬ

Carl and Betsy, another couple, had disagreed since their son Larry, now 14, had been an infant. Carl valued a person being assertive, even aggressive. He wanted his son to be able to take care of himself and to stand up for his rights. Betsy valued caring. She wanted her son to be considerate of others and to negotiate conflict nonviolently. She believed that war and killing were morally wrong. She felt that one step toward ending wars was to teach children to mediate their conflicts.

Betsy, with the other mothers in their church's play group, had worked with the children to help them be aware of others' needs as well as their own. They had taught the children to mediate their conflicts. In the early years at school the environment had been protective. Fighting was discouraged. The nonviolent techniques had worked.

On the soccer field and in Little League baseball Carl had encouraged his son to be assertive. "Go after the ball," he'd urged him. "Get out there and fight to win."

Carl felt his son was soft. He knew Larry could not stand up for himself. The summer before Larry was to enter high school, Carl brought the subject up again. He forced the issue of Larry's ability to protect himself physically because Larry was leaving the safer neighborhood middle school.

"We've got to talk about this, Bets. Larry is going to be in a school that tends to ignore how differences are handled until they get way out of hand. He is going to walk to school through neighborhoods where no one will be watching out for him. He needs to be more aggressive. He needs to be able to protect himself. He's a sitting duck now."

"It's not the way the neighborhood should be," Betsy protested.

"No, but it is the way it is," Carl stated firmly. "As I see it, we agree that we want Larry safe."

Betsy nodded, her head lowered.

"We know he has the nonviolent skills. He can continue working on them, using them first. But I think he needs to know other skills in case he needs them."

"Such as?" asked Betsy, looking up.

"Karate or some method of self-defense. They teach that karate is the method of last resort."

"That makes sense," Betsy said quietly.

When partners are aware

The partners of all three couples had sharp differences in their values for their children. Ken wanted immediate obedience, while Margo valued self-control. Jack wanted neatness and order, a value not high on Linda's list. Carl wanted an assertive child, able to stand up for his rights, even if it meant fighting. Betsy wanted one who would handle conflict nonviolently.

There were common features in the way the three couples dealt with their conflicts. All six partners were involved with their children and concerned about their welfare. These parents knew their values and the reasons for having them. Their reasons were answers to questions such as:

- Does this value represent for me a basic moral standard on which to base my life?
- Would the world be a better place if everyone lived by this principle?
- Will having this value lead to self-fulfillment?
- Who has set the value? Society, gender roles, civic responsibilities, family, or my needs?

The partners could articulate the reasons for holding the values they did. They also listened to each other, raised questions—even Jack and Linda did not storm out of the room. Listening to each other is so important, but it does not guarantee a resolution.

Finding common ground

The couples who were successful in resolving their conflicts were able to find a common ground of understanding. Ken realized that he valued having his child safe and able to assume responsibility for her toys more than he valued instant obedience. Betsy, like Carl, wanted her son to be safe and conceded that he needed to protect himself. If mediation did not work, Larry needed alternatives to resolve conflict.

These parents did not give up their values. They adapted them to life's realities, and they presented them at developmentally appropriate times. Nevertheless, their values remained unchanged. Larry would continue to try to resolve conflict nonviolently. Learning more about those skills and using them were part of his self-defense plan. Meanwhile, he was also going to learn how to protect himself physically. Amelia's parent's would challenge her to think about the consequences of her actions while continuing to keep her safe.

Parents can find ways to resolve many of the conflicts they find among their values. To do so takes openness, effort, and sometimes professional help. Use the questions on pages 169 and 171 to help you resolve conflicts between your own values and between yours and your partner's.

Tips for Resolving Conflicts

- Know your values and why they are important to you.
- Be aware of your differences.
- Explain your values to your partner.
- Listen to your partner's values and why they are important to him or her.
- Recognize differences in your perspectives.
- Find areas of agreement, such as common values on which to build, or the children's needs, or developmental influences, or any combination of areas.
- Be open to possible alternative ways of implementing your values.
- Be realistic about what you want your children to learn.

Teenagers
Need Values to Test

When children become teenagers parents have to change the way they think about integrating values into family life. In preceding chapters you have seen fourteen-year-old Steven balk at doing supper dishes alone, twelve-year-old Keith ignore his brother and sister and his friends, and Lynne worry about her thirteen- and sixteen-year olds, who might not deal with their grandfather's terminal illness very well. The behaviors of these teenagers reflect the new challenge their parents face.

Teen behavior is an expression of what is happening developmentally. Now with a basic knowledge of how their world works, teenagers start testing all over again whether the world *really* does work the way they have learned. In the process they question the basic values that have guided their lives since infancy. Do I want to safeguard my health? Is caring for others including my siblings necessary? Why should I clean up something I didn't mess up?

This change in their searching to understand comes because teenagers now have the ability to think abstractly. They can question and discuss almost everything from almost every angle. They talk out their questions. They also act them out. This exploring is part of their developmental task of establishing who they are and by what values they wish to live.

Your role in this process is to keep your teenager safe and to provide him with emotional support while helping him stay focused on the issues he is calling into question. What is the value involved with the issue? Is it your value and your teenager's? What are the implications of holding this value and of acting according to it?

Teenagers need the love, support, and guidance of their parents to

keep in touch with life as it really is and to have a secure base from which to question. You give your teenager a great gift when you are able to support his questioning while continuing to give him factual information and teach him relevant skills. This is not always an easy thing to do. Often in the process, parents themselves gain new insights.

ᦸᦸ

Mike banged the kitchen door, greeted his mother with a "Hi" followed by the question, "What's the difference between a good drug and a bad one?" He continued on his way to the refrigerator.

Bea, Mike's mother, took a deep breath. Mike had always been curious and was now at the stage where he was seeing connections between ideas he'd held for a long time. Bea never quite knew what to expect.

"What do you mean?" she asked.

"Well, a whole bunch of kids at school get Ritalin. They say it makes them feel good. The doctors prescribe it and it's okay. A lot of kids also smoke pot. They say it makes them feel good, too, but the doctors don't prescribe it and it's illegal. Is it the doctors who decide what's okay and what's not? How do they make that decision?"

"Actually, the doctors don't make the whole decision," answered Bea. She explained about the Federal Food and Drug Administration and its role in drug testing and approval.

She continued, "Some people do question the way doctors are prescribing Ritalin. I've heard psychologists wonder what the long-term effects are. I've heard teachers wonder if some children might not be better off learning how to focus. There are people who always recommend that counseling be given when the drug is. The use of drugs and staying healthy is complex."

By this time, Mike had the makings of a sandwich spread out on the counter and was busy putting together his snack.

"I don't know. It still doesn't make sense, though, that somebody can be arrested for having something like marijuana when people who are seriously ill like with AIDS or cancer feel it helps them."

"You realize," his mother started gently, as she got herself a cup of tea, "you're talking about two different uses. One is when people are dying with AIDS or cancer and one is when people want a recreational drug to make them feel good. Do you want some milk to go with your sandwich?"

"Well, what's the matter with wanting to feel good?"

"I didn't say there was anything the matter. I just pointed out the differences in use of the drugs," Bea said, putting down the glass of milk in front of Mike.

The two were silent for a while. Mike continued munching on his sandwich while his mother drank her tea.

"There are implications in that difference." Bea picked up on the theme, "If a sick person is taking a drug that will cause negative effects 10 years from now, but the disease will kill in two, that person doesn't have to be concerned about consequences the way a healthy person has to be."

"Are you saying that one shouldn't smoke marijuana because you don't know the long-term effects?" asked Mike.

"Marijuana and any other kind of drug, including ones prescribed by a doctor. You've heard me say that before," his mother added with a chuckle.

"Yeah, even about chewable vitamins. 'Only one. They're not candy, you know,'" Mike mimicked his mother. "Gosh, I've heard that as long as I can remember. But what would you say if I started smoking pot?"

"Hmm, I'd be very, very sad," Bea paused. "I'd worry about what you were doing to your health. I'd worry about long-term consequences. Adolescence is such an important time in a person's life to think through issues, just as you're doing now about drugs. I'm not sure a person using a lot of marijuana can do that kind of thinking. It's also illegal and you could get in serious trouble with the law. We know we can't stop you smoking elsewhere, but we wouldn't allow it here. We don't want the smell or the fumes in the house either. If you were old enough to drive, we would limit car use. And we'd watch the money. We're certainly not going to finance something that is potentially unhealthy for you and illegal, too. There would be other limits your dad and I would have to discuss."

Bea took a sip of tea before asking, "Are you being pressured? There must be an enticement if so many kids in school are doing it to know what smoking pot is like."

"Yeah. Kids on pot don't seem to worry. Like I've got this project to get finished. And I'm not sure I will. It'd be nice not to have my stomach in knots over it. Besides, they seem to have so much fun at parties."

"You feel out of it?" Bea questioned softly.

Mike nodded.

"I can remember feeling out of it at parties. Sometimes the kids did things I wasn't sure I wanted to do. It's hard not to go with the crowd or not to do what your friends do," said Bea.

Mike nodded again as he put his dirty dishes in the dishwasher, gathered up his book bag, and headed for his room.

Bea continued sitting at the counter after Mike had left. She thought about how she had continued to support her value of being healthy as she had analyzed it years ago (look at "Analyzing a Value" below). She felt comfortable now with how she had handled the conversation and the issues that had been left dangling. She wanted to remember to come back to the topic of needing to feel good and ways of doing so besides smoking marijuana. She knew that playing his trumpet was one way Mike could use, running another. He'd have some ideas, too. They'd have to talk more.

Analyzing a Value

HEALTHY

Thinking about the value

Definition: Physically and psychologically well; sound of mind and body; free from disease

Behavior reflecting value: He is able to function in daily living. He can enjoy being active physically. He likes mental challenges. He recovers balance when upset or disappointed or angry.

Knowledge and skills needed: He can read the needs of his body for rest, food, exercise, etc. He knows the difference between healthy and unhealthy, and knows how food, rest, and exercise affect health. He has skills that contribute to a healthy lifestyle, such as the ability to cook, read, play a sport, get information from a variety of sources.

Insights about the value: Keeping children healthy in our society is not easy due to such temptations as junk food and enticing activities that do not provide exercise. Establish healthful habits as early as possible.

Value present at birth? _X_ Yes ___No

Teaching or preserving the value

Baby: If he is healthy at birth, preserve that health by feeding healthy foods, helping him establish good sleeping habits, and keeping him clean. Encourage him to be in tune with his body by accepting his indication that he is full and not trying to get another ounce of milk into him and by recognizing when he is tired and putting him down for a nap. If he is not healthy, get appropriate medical attention and help him learn to cope with the challenges of his condition.

Toddler: Continue same care as for baby. Start potty training by helping child recognize when he needs to go. Help him avoid accidents while he is exploring his world: teach him to go down stairs feet first, help him learn how to be careful around hot things (liquids, heaters, fireplaces), and start teaching him to stay away from the street. Choose carefully the television programs he watches.

Preschool: Continue as with the toddler. Help him continue to be physically active. Start helping him learn to choose what television programs to watch. Limit the amount of time he watches television.

School age: Give him information about what makes a healthy diet, what sleep does for him, and how he can be in tune with his body. Teach him about the wise use of drugs, the reasons for abstaining from sex and having protected sex if abstention is not his choice later on, and how to deal with potentially harmful activities.

Teenage: Encourage him to listen to his body. Encourage healthy eating habits. Be open to discussing issues related to sex (abstention and protection), drugs, driving, smoking, abusive relationships, peer pressure, etc.

Influences on learning the value

Needs: The value of health determines how the needs are to be met. Meet his physiological needs in a manner that produces health: good food, plenty of rest, and so on. Protect him. For a child to be mentally healthy, he needs love, intellectual stimulation, and respect for who he is.

Temperament: If he is persistent and intense, he will find it harder to resist tempting foods such as candy, chips, soda pop. He is apt to need firmer guidelines. Helping him accommodate his body's demands for food and sleep on a regular schedule will be a major step in helping him learn to live a healthy life.

Learning style: Charts and diagrams related to healthy living will help a visual learner get the necessary information for well-being. Modeling appropriate behavior and including him in activities will help him if he learns by doing. Talking about health is helpful if he learns by listening.

Reflections about the value

Influence of other values: Thoughtful decision making is imperative to his ability to live a healthy life.

New thinking resulting from analysis: Throughout life children and adults must make decisions about what they eat, how much they sleep, how much exercise to get, whether to use drugs, how they drive, whether to rest or go to school/work when they do not feel well. Their decisions affect their health and may have long-term consequences. Therefore, parents and children have to learn and teach healthy living for as long as they live.

TEENAGERS BUILD
PERSONAL VALUE SYSTEMS

Adolescence is the stage of life when young people begin to decide which values they want to guide their lives. Now beginning to be able to think abstractly, they are capable of questioning the values by which they have lived so far. Mike is able to start to deal with issues such as the difference between Ritalin and marijuana, and how society views the two through its laws. Underlying the questions he asked was a more personal one: If I value my health, how am I going to use drugs? As a younger child, he had just accepted that one drug was viewed as all right and the other as not.

One of the dangers for teenagers is that they can see the inconsistencies of positions that adults take, as in cigarette use, for example. Teenagers are told not to take up smoking, but they see adults smoking and they are targeted with sophisticated advertising that encourages them to smoke. As a consequence of seeing the inconsistencies, many teenagers discount all values and act accordingly.

Parents who have been concerned that they should not be setting values for their children can relax. Most children will ultimately decide their values for themselves. It is during adolescence that they begin to do so. Having a strong value system to question and argue against gives them a firm basis on which to create their own.

COMMUNICATING WITH TEENAGERS

There were several features of Mike and his mother's discussion that must have made it more useful for Mike. One was the obvious rapport between the two, shown by Mike's offhanded greeting and his immediate plunge into the question.

Another was the freedom both obviously felt to raise issues and ask questions. Mike stated his question about drugs in a very straightforward, open manner. Bea, in her turn, asked why the question had come up at this time.

The discussion occurred within a history of valuing health and following healthy patterns. Mike's parents had thought through issues related to health. Mike had grown up with people who valued his health. Consequently, he knew his mother's position on the issue of drugs: "Vitamins are not candy. Take only one a day." He knew the reason for the rule was to protect children's health. This discussion was one of many that had occurred in various ways as Mike was growing up. When he was a baby and toddler, drugs were kept out of reach. At ages 3 and 4, Mike learned that his mother followed the doctor's prescription exactly. In elementary school, he had become aware of when his parents took drugs and under what conditions. He also learned that some drugs were illegal and others obtainable only through prescription. Now, he is questioning the whole system. His basic value, however, has not changed. He wants to stay healthy.

Also, Mike felt he could trust his mother for information. Even with his mother's position on drugs, Mike seemed to assume he could get straight answers. His trust was realistic. She gave him not only honest answers, but ones that described the complexity of the issues. An example

---

How to Talk to a Teenager

• Have a positive, established relationship to start with.
  This consists of:
      Rapport between the two of you,
      Trust that any question can be raised and will be answered
      as accurately as possible,
      A child raised by value-guided parenting.
• Keep discussion open and nonconfrontational by:
      Giving factual information
      Clarifying statements made by either of you
      Diffusing challenges
      Keeping focused
      Dealing with feelings
      Staying calm
• Know your values.
• Plan for a follow-up discussion to take care of loose ends.

---

is her mention of the different positions authorities currently take on pre-scribing Ritalin.

Bea handled the discussion in a way that kept it open and allowed her to support her values and her son's exploring. She clarified his statements, "You realize you are talking about two different uses." She defused his challenges. When Mike challenged her that she was criticizing wanting to feel good, she restated her position, "I didn't say there was anything the matter. I just pointed out the differences in use." She then went on to explain those differences objectively and specifically. She kept him focused. "Are you being pressured?" she asked after a pause. She dealt with his feelings, "You feel out of it?" and "It's hard." She built a bond by letting him know she knew a little of what he was experiencing. She also pointed out that marijuana use is illegal.

Bea recognized that this discussion was one of many. She planned for the next by thinking about what had not been said and needed to be. She wanted to remind Mike of ways he had of dealing with stress that were healthier and safer than smoking marijuana, as well as legal.

The nonconfrontational approach of both Mike and his mother made this discussion possible. Mike was seeking information and did not feel he had to defend a position. Bea discussed the issue without making a judgmental statement about what was right or wrong or about the children at school, and she did not jump to the conclusion that Mike was already doing something she did not want him to do. This kind of verbal exploring is vital for teenagers. Being able to explore questions with a trusted adult who knows them well, as well as with friends, teachers, and others who may be available, puts the teenager in a better position to face the issues squarely.

DISCUSSIONS CAN BE DIFFICULT

Unfortunately, for many parents, a discussion about such sensitive subjects as drugs often does not proceed so easily. People are or become defensive. Instead of Mike's easy opening question, he might have said, "Laws against marijuana just don't make sense. Look at all the Ritalin that is handed out. It works on the mind, too. I don't know why you all make such big deal about it. I am going to that party and I will smoke marijuana. It's the only way to make the party fun."

Or Mike could have dismissed the value of health, as in, "Why worry about my health? We'll all be dead before I'm 50 anyhow. Someone will blow us up. Let's have fun now."

Or Mike's mother could have responded to Mike's laid back opening question about the difference between legal and illegal drugs with, "Well, the government has this board that tests drugs. They keep us safe. They have found drugs like marijuana to be unsafe."

"But, Mom," Mike could have said, "Ritalin works on your mind, too."

"But that drug has been tested and found to benefit many people, particularly children," she could have answered.

With some assertive young people, it is possible to defuse their argument by repeatedly working to keep it an open discussion. Hearing her child's rampage against the law and the plan to use marijuana, a parent might ask, if the topic had not come up before, "That's a strong statement. What raised this issue for you now?" Or if it were a continuing discussion, a parent might ask, "Sounds like a party coming up. Whose?" and "Who will be there?" or "Are you telling me what to expect when you come in Saturday night?"

For many parents it takes practice to think ahead of ways of holding to their values and yet helping their children explore an issue. Having already thought through the issues related to the value helps a great deal. Mike's mother could state the dilemma and her belief.

If your teenager is actually involved in the behavior and has already shifted in his values, you have a different set of issues. You have to decide how far you will tolerate the behavior or bend in accepting it and what you will do if the activity is illegal. In the case of marijuana, the limits might be those Bea spoke of: "No smoking in the house," "No driving the car. We will come and get you," "If you drive you lose car privileges," "Keep your grades up," "If you bring the stuff into the house we may have to ask you to leave. We have to think of the other children," "It is illegal—we don't want you to use it."

In extreme situations the issue may come to focus on the relationship itself. How far will or can you bend to keep in contact with your child? How much are you willing and able to overlook while the child figures out her position? Starting with a strong relationship between you and your child is a major advantage. It helps to carry the relationship through the turbulent times or perhaps return to it after the crisis, though it is no guarantee.

PARENTS CAN HAVE A ROLE

Parents can continue to have a role in their children's evolving value system. They can be open to discuss any issue the child raises—drugs, sex, the war in _____ (you fill in the blank), the impact of a pregnancy on a fifteen-year-old at school, the collection of guns in their best friend's house, the fact that there is poverty in a wealthy nation, the contradictions between what people say and what they do. Such discussions are one way teenagers build their value systems.

The parental role changes in its emphasis from when the child was younger. With younger children your role was that of being a source of information about a value. In adolescence your role focuses more on helping your child explore the implications of a value.

You can help your teenager view directly the inconsistencies of values in society, and sort out the differences among your family value system, the peer culture one, and society's. In the process, you will be helping your teenager evolve the value system by which he or she will live.

A strong relationship with your teenager will make it easier to guide him through the adolescent years. Bea and Mike had developed over time their rapport, freedom to ask questions, and trust. They had a history of integrating values into their lives and of discussing those values.

The role is a difficult one for parents. It is hard to listen to children take all kinds of positions, to help them see the advantages and disadvantages of each, and still hold to your values. Mike's mother could see the dilemma and still state her position on drugs.

PARENTS MAY NEED TO RETHINK VALUES

Sometimes you must recognize that one or more of your values are no longer valid, or your behavior no longer supports a value. Teenagers trying to figure out by what values they wish to live can make you renew your own search.

One family with teenagers encountered this situation over the issue of food. Their teenagers' college years coincided with the health food movement. A generation earlier, when their own mother had come home from college, their grandmother would prepare her daughter's favorite foods of steak, mashed potatoes, and gravy. Now when the teenagers came home, they wanted to take over the kitchen. They hoped to find tofu, woks, and lots of fresh fruits, vegetables, and no red meats: "But, Mom, red meat isn't good for you." They would recite the information. They made their parents face the fact that the way they were integrating healthy living was no longer considered healthy. Adolescence can also be a time of parental change and growth.

Adolescence is a time when teenagers question the values by which they have been raised and of deciding which values will guide their lives. Teenagers not only question, they all too often act, which increases parents' concerns for both their child and for others around them. You can have a vital role as consultant with whom teenagers can express their changing opinions and from whom they can get a consistently thoughtful response. Parents who have a close relationship with their teenagers are in a good position to warn them when behavior might become dangerous and to set limits when it does.

Parents who know their values will be more effective in their role of consultant. You can name your values as well as describe what they mean and why they are important. You have thought through the implications of the values and can discuss them. You can even change the implications knowingly. You can use your values, as the sailor uses the stars, to guide your children on the way to fulfilling, enriching lives.

Reflecting on Family Life

What were your reactions to Mike and Bea's discussion about drugs? Think about the last discussion *you* had with *your* teenager in which values were a part.
• How did your teenager hear your concerns?
• Which of Bea's methods of handling the conversation and the issues did you use?
• Which of her methods might you try in the next discussion with your teenager?
• How would you like to "go back and do it again" if you had the opportunity?

Epilogue

The other day I ran into Bianca in the supermarket.

"Harriet, how are you?" she greeted me with a chuckle. "Derek and I were just talking about you and the values we selected in that parenting discussion group . . . I think it must be fifteen years ago."

"It's good to see you, Bianca," I returned warmly. "Sean must be . . . "

"Nineteen."

"Goodness," I shook my head, "it doesn't seem possible."

"I have to tell you something. Sean is going to be a camp counselor this summer. He's very excited. He came home from college at spring break wanting to talk with us. He'd just found out he's going to have the youngest campers. He asked us, 'What would you think if I wrote them and found out something about them before they came . . . what they like to do? Then I could have activities planned that they'd enjoy and maybe they'd be less homesick.'

"Now, isn't that a great example of caring? After Sean left, Derek and I got to reminiscing—that's where you came in—how we'd wanted the boys to be caring, how we'd worked with Sean to help him relate to his younger brother. It all seems to be paying off. We feel so good about how the boys are turning out."

"You should feel good," I responded enthusiastically. "You worked hard to keep that spirit of caring alive."

"And it seemed so outlandish," continued Bianca, "back when he was a little guy to think that helping him learn how to touch his new brother was working toward a value as important as caring. But Derek and I traced several of the steps. Our value guided our way."

My wish for all you parents is that you too will be so blessed 10 or 15 or 20 years from now to see in your children those values that you hold dear and that have served as your guides through your child-rearing years.

Analyzing a Value

Analyzing a Value

AFFECTIONATE

Thinking about the value

Definition: Feeling warm regard towards others; friendly

Behavior reflecting value: He can express his affection through hugs, touches, choice of words, and tone of voice. He greets a friend with a warm hug; snuggles up to his parent for a story; describes someone's strengths; voices concerns gently regarding someone else's feelings.

Knowledge and skills needed: He needs to know when being affectionate is appropriate and when it is not. Needs to learn how to hear his own words and tone of voice when he is speaking of another and how he sounds when he expresses regard appropriately. He needs to be sensitive to how another person is responding.

Insights about the value: In the United States we live in a culture that tends not to be affectionate. Our babies are carried around in rigid plastic carriers for the most part. We tend to speak harshly to children. For boys, it is often considered unmanly to be affectionate. During their elementary school years boys often withdraw from expressing any kind of affection. Nowadays, with sexual abuse on the rise and reported more readily, parents are often confused about how to express appropriate affection to their teenagers, particularly those of the opposite sex. Yet teenagers, too, need to receive and express affection. Throughout a child's development, then, parents must work to build and preserve affection in their child.

Value present at birth?___Yes ___No That depends on the definition of affectionate. A new baby certainly knows how to mold his body to his mother's as she holds him. Other physical expressions of affection usually develop rapidly in a baby who is loved and hugged.

Teaching or preserving the value

Baby: Most babies thrive on being held, touched, and paid attention to. They become more animated. Within the first two months of life a baby begins to look for affection and respond to smiles, cooing, and snuggling. As he grows, he learns to give affection by hugging and kissing and doing for his care givers what they do for him (offering bites of food or covering them up, for example).

Toddler: Even as he becomes more independent and moves around on his own, he returns to adults to get and to give hugs and kisses. As he starts to talk, encourage him to use kindly words and tone of voice. Model the tone of voice and body language you wish him to mimic (learn). Gently let him know how you are feeling, and assure him that you like his hugs, too.

Preschooler: As he moves out of the home to visit friends, go to day care and/or preschool, establish routines of expressing affection, such as hugs and kisses on greeting and separating, in the morning and before bed, and upon seeing relatives and friends. Continue to help him know how others are feeling, how different tones of voice sound, and how to control the tone of his own voice.

School age: Continue with what is appropriate from the earlier age. Give good-bye hugs and kisses in private at this age, instead of in front of other children at the bus stop. The important point is to continue giving them. Take advantage of other times to offer and receive affection—while reading, watching television, or just having a conversation together. Continue to help him hear himself so that he learns how an imperious, demanding tone makes parents (and others) feel put down and unappreciated. Let him know that his hugs and kisses are important to you.

Teenage: Continue the above. Teenagers very much need to receive and give those hugs. These must be appropriate and kindly. Working on kindly communication is difficult at this developmental stage, so just try to keep the idea subtly present.

Influences on learning the value

Needs: When the physiological needs and those for protection have been satisfied, his intense social needs of wanting to love and be loved will motivate him to be affectionate and to learn how to express affection.

Temperament: Some children are highly sensitive to touch. They will fuss, even cry and pull away. If you have a child like this, you will quite logically feel rejected. For most of these children, there are ways to work around the sensitivity. You may need help, first to realize that he is not rejecting you and then to figure out how to make contact with him.

Learning style: If he does not hear subtle differences in sound, he may need more help learning how to control his tone of voice.

Reflections about the value

Influence of other values: Both his ability to be aware and to care will help him know how to be appropriately affectionate.

New thinking resulting from analysis: Cultural influences undermine this value. It will take hard work for a family to keep alive the expressions of affection that members have for one another.

Analyzing a Value
AWARE

~~~~~~~~~~

Thinking about the value

Definition: Open to what is going on around one; having intensified perceptions; noticing details

Behavior reflecting value: She notices when someone looks unhappy. She recognizes changes in the landscape. She hears the change in a person's tone of voice. She understands the unspoken meanings in what people say.

Knowledge and skills needed: She must be able to feel, see, hear, touch, and remember.

Insights about the value: A child's awareness can vary from totally unaware to overly sensitive. You have to decide how much awareness needs to be taught, and what kind: beauty of nature? kindness of others? feelings of playmates? You must also decide how to introduce awareness of the unpleasant facts of life, such as starvation, war, violence, effects of natural disasters, etc.

Value present at birth? _X_ Yes ___No

Teaching or preserving the value

Baby: Give her an interesting environment to look at, touch, taste, listen to, and manipulate. Keep her safe as she explores. Give her the words for what she is doing as she does it. Acknowledge her feelings and give her words for feelings, too. Grant her time: time in which to grow and develop as well as time to be with her parents.

Toddler: Give her the same experiences as baby. Provide new opportunities to explore, such as other people's homes, the grocery store, playgrounds, natural areas, the library, Mom or Dad's office. As she becomes able, encourage her to talk about her experiences, what she does, hears, and sees. Give her more words, including abstract ones, such as for feelings.

Preschool and school age: Continue giving opportunities to experience things, with ever-widening scope, keeping aware of both her interests and her lack of experience. Support her in those experiences that are sad or tragic for her. Answer her questions with accurate information and discuss issues important to her. Help her learn to find answers for herself.

Teenage: At this stage, she becomes aware of abstract concepts such as ethics, morality, double standards, contradictions between word and deed. Continue to support her exploration and encourage her awareness, even of painful or frightening ideas and experiences.

Influences on learning the value

Needs: An extremely sensitive child's needs to feel safe and protected can be taxing. Be particularly careful not to overburden such a child and help her learn how to deal with her sensitivities. If she is unaware, she can be oblivious to potential danger, so you must work to keep her safe.

Temperament: If she has high sensory awareness, she will be more aware of what is going on around her. Acknowledge her experiences and give her words to describe them. If she is oblivious, coach her and point things out to her, describing what she sees happening.

Learning style: If she has a strong preference for either auditory or visual learning and is also oblivious, teach her in her preferred learning style how to be aware. For example, if she is unaware that her friend wants to play, say, "Julia wants to play with you. See how she has come over to you and is offering to share her toy?"

Reflections about the value

Influence of other values: To be aware requires energy and alertness. A child will need to be healthy, well-nourished, and rested in order to be aware of what is happening around her.

New thinking resulting from analysis: It would be very easy to shut off a child's awareness of what is going on around her by preventing her from exploring and by denying what she experiences. A very aware child could also be easily overwhelmed in today's world.

A

Analyzing a Value

Caring, able to care

~~~~~~~~~~

Thinking about the value

Definition: Able to feel, think, and act in the interests of others, oneself, and the environment

Behavior reflecting value: He picks up litter by the side of the road; fixes a snack willingly for a younger sibling; reads to an elderly neighbor whose eyesight is failing. He refuses to take drugs. He makes sure pets have food, water, exercise, and shelter.

Knowledge and skills needed: He can brainstorm ideas. He can recognize the need for relevant knowledge and skills, and has the ability to seek them out. He has the skills needed to put caring into action. He can make decisions based on caring as a value, and he can plan and carry out his plan.

Insights about the value: Behaving in a caring way relies heavily on wanting to do so and having the appropriate information and skills. Decision-making skills are particularly important.

Value present at birth?___Yes __X_No

Teaching or preserving the value

Baby: Teach him to differentiate between living and nonliving things. Help him interact with other people. Help him experience consequences in the natural world by providing safe opportunities, such as having him hold something very warm while you say "hot."

Toddler: Provide opportunities for him to be around other people, including babies and other toddlers. Help him learn that humans must be touched differently from objects, that they cry and can be hurt, and that they are particularly fun to be with.

Preschool: Help him learn to take turns and then to share, and that others have feelings similar to his own. Continue to provide opportunities for him to interact with other people. Give him a chance to entertain a younger child and to care for the environment (picking up trash at the playground or while taking a walk, for example).

School age: Encourage him to recognize the need for information about what he is going to care for—younger child, pet, plant, etc.—and the need for skills to put his caring into action. Teach him how to get information and skills. Help him understand how another person may think and feel differently than he does. Talk about how people differ and how their needs differ as a result. Discuss how to plan to care for a younger child for a short time, maybe by reading a story or playing a game. Talk about how to care for the environment.

Teenage: Provide opportunities for him to care for something. By this age he should be able to be involved, take another's perspective, find out the needs of the person or thing being cared for, understand the situation, and make plans. He should possess skills to put caring into action or know how to acquire them. If he does not have the skills, which is very possible given that our culture does not emphasize caring, you may need to provide opportunities for him to learn. **Note:** Developmental tasks of teenagers frequently interfere with the ability to care for other people or things. On the other hand, teenagers are often the most altruistic of people.

Influences on learning the value

Needs: His social needs will provide some motivation for him to want to learn how to care for others, including pets.

Temperament: If he is emotionally sensitive, he will be aware of how another is feeling, which gives him useful information when he wants to care for another person. A child who is very focused on his own affairs and is not a strong "people" person has more difficulty thinking about the needs of others.

Learning style: A visual learner needs visual clues, so books, pictures, and charts are helpful in teaching what is involved in caring for someone or something, like a pet.

Reflections about the value

Influence of other values: Thoughtful decision making is important in dealing with a situation in which we plan to care for someone or something. Information and relevant skills are necessary. A child needs to learn when it is appropriate to care and when it is more important to base his behavior on other values, such as assertiveness, competitiveness, or attention to his own needs.

New thinking resulting from analysis: Acting in a caring way requires more than the simple desire to be helpful. It is a complex process, requiring motivation, knowledge, and skills.

Analyzing a Value

Cooperative

Thinking about the value

Definition: Act and work with others for mutual benefit or for a common purpose. Able to work as part of a team.

Behavior reflecting value: Two children who have one wagon figure out a way they can both use it. Children involved in a school group project figure out an equal work load for each member and all complete their assignments. High school students working on the student newspaper recognize each member's strengths and organize the tasks to make use of these strengths.

Knowledge and skills needed: People must have the desire to cooperate. To be able to cooperate requires various kinds of knowledge and skills based upon the situation. It also demands that he be able to recognize the task requiring cooperation to complete. He must know the issues involved where cooperation is expected. He needs to have the skills to know how to negotiate the completion of the necessary tasks.

Insights about the value: There is a process to cooperating:

- Acknowledge that there is a task to be done and recognize that cooperation will facilitate accomplishing it.
- Possess knowledge about the task, what needs to be done, how it needs to be done, and what skills are involved.
- Know who will be cooperating and what their strengths and skills are.
- Draw up a plan, pairing what needs to be done with the strengths of those who will do the task.
- Carry out the plan during which the cooperation will take place.

Value present at birth?____Yes __X__No

Teaching or preserving the value

Baby: A very early stage in learning to cooperate occurs when baby and parent take turns cooing at each other. The mutual goal is to communicate: both learn to initiate the task, to respond, and to take turns.

Toddler: Teach him to take turns: he has the toy for two minutes, then someone else has it for two minutes. The task is to play together and have fun; the skill is knowing how to share. He will be motivated to continue sharing, even though his needs and desires at this stage are very demanding, because he is having such a good time.

Preschool: He has many experiences in cooperation as he negotiates with others who is to play what role in the doll corner or how to build the castle in the block corner. His task is to have fun with others. The skill he is learning is negotiation (who will be whom). Help him learn to cooperate on household tasks by stating the task and then showing him how to do it: "There is no space to play here with all these blocks scattered around. Here, let's stack them in the corner."

School age: Team sports give children wonderful opportunities to cooperate. Unfortunately, adults usually do the organizing. A child needs opportunities to plan what needs to be done and who is to do what (with consideration of each person's strengths). He needs help learning the necessary negotiating skills. All members of a team need to do their share of the work and rewards need to take into consideration that each member has done his or her part. **Note:** Teachers should not allow shirking. Those children are learning, not how to cooperate, but how to manipulate the system, while the children who do the work are experiencing cooperation as unfair.

Teenage: Teenagers need many opportunities to work cooperatively together on meaningful tasks. Parents' and teachers' challenge continues to be to assure that all team members (siblings, for example) are assuming their share of the load.

Influences on learning

Needs: Conditions of great need for food and/or protection may motivate people to cooperate. Under less critical conditions, people's needs to be social, to belong, will motivate them to be cooperative. Therefore, make sure his needs for self-esteem and personal achievement are satisfied so that his drive for cooperation is not diminished.

Temperament: Some children who tend to become very involved in a task have trouble taking the time to negotiate; they also may have trouble letting others do their part. Such children may also be perfectionists and be unwilling to accept work that is less well done. Figure out where your child falls on the spectrum.

Learning style: A visual learner needs to see how a task will be done. He may function slower in groups than if he were more of a listener. Visual learners may even need to diagram how the work will be accomplished.

Reflections about the value

Influence of other values: Being aware of what is happening in a group and how individuals are responding can give him insights into how to make the cooperative effort more fruitful. He needs to be a thoughtful, reflective thinker, also.

New thinking resulting from analysis: There is so much knowledge and so many skills relevant to both the task to be done and to the skill of cooperating. Sharing is a step on the way. Expecting a child to do a household task is not teaching him to set up a cooperative situation. He needs experience in thinking through what needs to be done, who can do it, when it should be done, and how people are going to work together to get it done.

Sometimes parents say, "Cooperate with me," when what they really want is obedience, as in "Do this now."

Analyzing a Value

CURIOUS

Thinking about the value

Definition: Having the desire to figure out; to understand

Behavior reflecting value: A toddler takes a bite of rhubarb, and then another, and another, each time with an expression that indicates she wonders if that bite will be the same as the last one. A nine-year-old wonders why Mars has a reddish haze and looks in the encyclopedia for information. A microbiologist spends her life studying viruses. (People whose curiosity has been kept alive become self-educating.)

Knowledge and skills needed: Her awareness of the details in the environment and her understanding of how they relate to each other provides the basis for her curiosity. She needs skills, such as how to pose a question and then how to find the answer. Someone like the microbiologist needs specialized skills to enable her to search for answers in highly specialized fields.

Insights about the value: Children are born curious. It is necessary for survival. Children learn because they are curious. Use her curiosity to help her learn many of the things she needs to know to live a fulfilling life.

However, curiosity can be killed easily. You can destroy it by not allowing her to explore, by overstimulating her with too much to explore, by not allowing her to explore at her own pace, and even by not assuring her of satisfaction that she has gained at least some increased understanding of whatever she is interested in. You need to work to keep her curiosity alive.

Value present at birth? _X_ Yes ___No

Teaching or preserving the value

Baby: She is displaying curiosity as she looks at, listens to, touches, smells, and tastes her environment. She satisfies her curiosity through her senses. Give her things to look at, reach out for, and manipulate. Let her touch your face, hair, and body. As she starts to crawl, encourage her to explore her living space and the outdoors. Tell her what she is experiencing because babies start learning language immediately upon being born.

Toddler: Allow her to continue to explore, and offer her even more and new opportunities. Give her words for what she is doing: "Look, you opened the cabinet door." Let her struggle to figure out how to do something, let her experiment with how things work. After she has experimented swinging the gate back and forth and standing on both sides of it and walking through it, then give her words: "The gate swings back and forth. It lets us go through the fence." Use discipline techniques that help her understand cause and effect.

Preschool: Continue as for the toddler. Also, take note of what draws her interest and build on that interest with books, the library, the Internet, other people with knowledge, field trips, etc. Change your focus as you see her interests change.

School age: Continue exploring with her to help her find answers to her questions and teach her how to find answers. Discuss what she learns with her. Be aware of what is going on in her school. Schools can be excellent sources of encouragement and assistance, but dull lessons and rigid curricula can also stifle a child's curiosity. As a parent, your role is to be aware of what is happening and how she responds to it. Act as her advocate for more appropriate learning situations and/or develop and support her interests outside school. Many a child's inborn curiosity has been saved in spite of the school system by an attentive parent's willingness to listen and to help find interesting materials.

Teenage: She should be able to ask questions and develop a strategy for finding answers about issues that are straightforward. However, she may also be asking questions by now for which there are no answers yet and she may begin to think about getting the specialized skills needed to find the answers she wants.

Influences on learning the value

Needs: Curiosity is a basic need. When the physiological needs and those for protection are met, people's curiosity motivates them to want to know and understand. The search for knowledge, satisfying one's curiosity, is very self-fulfilling for many people.

Temperament: Children who are distractible and/or not persistent will have greater trouble searching out answers. They want instant replies or become distracted with some other activity. If she is like this, you must follow a fine line. With the distractible child, your challenge is to bring her back to the original interest without turning her off. With a child who is not persistent, your challenge is to get her to keep pursuing her interests without turning off her curiosity.

Learning style: When she is young, she should be encouraged to explore using all her senses. If she has a strong mode of learning, her exploration will undoubtedly take place mostly in that mode. With the kinesthetic (movement) learner, she may have to build a tree fort and get her supplies up and down via rope and basket in order to learn about gravity, instead of reading about it.

Reflections about the value

Influence of other values: Her curiosity may adversely affect her caring for others and for the property of others. It may not be prudent to take an exploring toddler visiting or shopping where there are breakables within her reach.

Her sense of right and wrong—her value system—will determine how she uses the knowledge she seeks out. Part of the process of answering questions and discussing issues with an older child is to bring up relevant ethical questions, even, or maybe especially, if they are difficult to answer.

New thinking resulting from analysis: Thinking through this value shows that a large part of curiosity is being self-educating. Curiosity is not just about wanting to know something, it is also about being able to find out about it, that is, self-educating.

Analyzing a Value
Healthy

Thinking about the value

Definition: Physically and psychologically well; sound of mind and body; free from disease

Behavior reflecting value: He is able to function in daily living. He can enjoy being active physically. He likes mental challenges. He recovers balance when upset or disappointed or angry.

Knowledge and skills needed: He can read the needs of his body for rest, food, exercise, etc. He knows the difference between healthy and unhealthy, and knows how food, rest, and exercise affect health. He has skills that contribute to a healthy lifestyle, such as the ability to cook, read, play a sport, get information from a variety of sources.

Insights about the value: Keeping children healthy in our society is not easy due to such temptations as junk food and enticing activities that do not provide exercise. Establish healthful habits as early as possible.

Value present at birth? X Yes ___No

Teaching or preserving the value

Baby: If he is healthy at birth, preserve that health by feeding healthy foods, helping him establish good sleeping habits, and keeping him clean. Encourage him to be in tune with his body by accepting his indication that he is full and by recognizing when he is tired and putting him down for a nap. If he is not healthy, get appropriate medical attention and help him learn to cope with the challenges of his condition.

Toddler: Continue same care as for baby. Start potty training by helping child recognize when he needs to go. Help him avoid accidents while he is exploring his world: teach him to go down stairs feet first, help him learn how to be careful around hot things, and start teaching him to stay away from the street. Choose carefully the television programs he watches.

Preschool: Continue as with the toddler. Help him be physically active. Start helping him learn to choose what television programs to watch.

School age: Give him information about what makes a healthy diet, what sleep does for him, and how he can be in tune with his body. Teach him about the wise use of drugs, the reasons for abstaining from sex and having protected sex if abstention is not his choice later on, and how to deal with potentially harmful activities.

Teenage: Encourage him to listen to his body. Encourage healthy eating habits. Be open to discussing issues related to sex (abstention and protection), drugs, driving, smoking, abusive relationships, peer pressure, etc.

Influences on learning the value

Needs: The value of health determines how the needs are to be met. Meet his physiological needs in a manner that produces health: good food, plenty of rest, and so on. Protect him. For a child to be mentally healthy, he needs love, intellectual stimulation, and respect for who he is.

Temperament: If he is persistent and intense, he will find it harder to resist tempting foods such as candy, chips, soda pop. He is apt to need firmer guidelines. Helping him accommodate his body's demands for food and sleep on a regular schedule will be a major step in helping him learn to live a healthy life.

Learning style: Charts and diagrams related to healthy living will help a visual learner get the necessary information for well-being. Modeling appropriate behavior and including him in activities will help him if he learns by doing. Talking about health is helpful if he learns by listening.

Reflections about the value

Influence of other values: Thoughtful decision making is imperative to his ability to live a healthy life.

New thinking resulting from analysis: Throughout life children and adults must make decisions about what they eat, how much they sleep, how much exercise to get, whether to use drugs, how they drive, whether to rest or go to school/work when they do not feel well. Their decisions affect their health and may have long-term consequences. Parents and children have to learn and teach healthy living for as long as they live.

Analyzing a Value
HONEST

~~~~~~~~~~~~~~~~

Thinking about the value

Definition: To tell the truth; to live based on truth

Behavior reflecting value: She tells the truth at all times, under every circumstance. She admits to eating the candy, though she knew she was supposed to wait until after dinner. She reports the auto accident exactly as it happened, even if she was at fault. She does not commit verbally to one thing and then do another.

Knowledge and skills needed: To be honest, she must be aware of what is happening and remember it accurately. She must be in touch with reality.

Insights about the value: To be in touch with reality is a developmental trait. Children younger than five or six have trouble keeping reality separate from what they wish for or what they pretend. They do not yet have the thinking skills to do so. Therefore, to expect young children to be "honest" is unrealistic. They do not understand the concept.

Honesty also takes courage. It is often difficult to recognize and then admit to oneself or to someone else that one did not handle a situation well, or did not do what one should have done. A child can only develop that kind of courage in an atmosphere of trust, where she knows she is safe.

Value present at birth? ___ Yes _X_ No

Teaching or preserving the value

Baby: The concept of honesty has no meaning for a baby. At this stage, she is building her concept of the world. It is important for her to experience the world as having structure and routine, where her needs will be met. This will give her a basis on which honesty can be built when she is older.

Toddler/Preschool: To expect honesty of children between age two and six is unrealistic because of their cognitive development. Give your child a sense of what is real and true and give her something to build on as she grows by reviewing a situation for her—you do have to provide the review. This is why parents and teachers of toddlers and preschoolers need to stay aware of everything, how the play is going, who is doing what, and so on, because the children cannot give us accurate information when things go wrong. They cannot yet differentiate between the real and the imagined, between what happened and what they wish happened.

School age/Teenage: Children at this age are able to tell the difference between what happened and what they wish had happened. You have a unique role to play in helping her face reality and tell the truth. There are several challenges.

Follow her activities enough to know what is going on and when she is telling the truth or not. During the teenage years this can be very difficult because so much of what teens do is out of the home. Two things to do are keep in touch with other parents and know what her school expects of her.

Another challenge is to be sure to take time to listen carefully to and understand her side of an issue. Do not make threats of punishment so severe that she is afraid to tell the truth. Also, be sure to let a child who is lying know that she is still loved and cherished even though she is lying, and that you expect her to change and start telling the truth. Be careful not to label her a liar because labels promote the behavior they describe.

Influences on learning the value

Needs: The drive to meet most needs can interfere with a person's ability to be honest. A starving person may steal food and lie about doing so. She may lie to protect herself or a friend from harm or to protect her own or a friend's self-esteem. In many situations it takes courage to be honest, which is perhaps why the two qualities are so often linked.

Temperament: No relevance.

Learning style: Some children have poor memories: they either do not remember what happened or remember it inaccurately. These children need special protection and gentle reminding of what did occur. For a parent or a teacher to call such a child a liar is to accuse her unfairly.

Reflections about the value

Influence of other values: Raw, straightforward honesty can get in the way of a caring response or cooperative effort. Uncle Joe might not be destitute if he had handled his money more wisely, but her telling him so does not show a caring concern for his well-being, even if it is honest. Likewise, reminding someone she did not cooperate on the last project is not going to get her to cooperate on a new project; better to keep it in mind and help the group of which she is a part organize the new project with clearer expectations.

New thinking resulting from analysis: In analyzing being honest, it is evident that the value is more complex than a simple answer of this or that happened, this person did this or that. Caring for the well-being of someone else or seeking to build a cooperative effort may mean using knowledge of the truth to do something differently, without stating the truth or accusing someone else.

Knowing that your child has smoked marijuana or is sexually active may mean that what is important is protecting her and stating your concern for her, rather than getting her to admit to you what she has done. She does not need to acknowledge unsafe activity in order to accept help and protection from you. In this case, the goal of keeping your child safe may conflict with your value of honesty.

Analyzing a Value

INTELLIGENT

~~~~~~~~~

Thinking about the value

Definition: Having a wide range of knowledge and/or great depth of knowledge in specific fields. Information is available for appropriate use. Common usage of the term usually applies to academic endeavors.

We recognize that there are different kinds of intelligence, too. Among these are social, musical, athletic, mathematical, verbal, spatial, etc., meaning that people may have particular aptitude for acquiring knowledge in one of these areas. Wisdom, in contrast to intelligence, is having knowledge and being able to use it wisely in everyday life.

Behavior: Child can explain in detail some natural happening, such as earthquakes or metamorphosis. Adult can converse about a large range of topics. Child does well academically. She receives high scores on intelligence tests and measures of academic achievement, such as the SAT. She often has a large vocabulary.

Knowledge and skills: Intelligence is based on having information and having the skills to use it appropriately—in other words, being able to think and to express those thoughts. Expression may be through the written word, musical composition, art, etc.

Insights about the value: Intelligence develops in a warm, loving, supportive relationship. All children, even the most intelligent, need guidance and direction. They all go through the developmental stages outlined in chapter six. It is especially easy to assume that highly verbal children understand a situation better than they do. Listen carefully to your seemingly knowledgeable young child to stay in touch with her level of comprehension. Remember your teenager's lack of experience, no matter how sophisticated she sounds, when you guide her.

Value present at birth?___Yes   _X_ No The potential for intelligence exists at birth.

Teaching or preserving the value

Baby: Interact and play with baby. Give her many opportunities to interact with other people and objects. She uses all her senses during this period of exploration. Talk to her about what she is doing and discovering. Follow her interests and reactions. Maintain a balance between enough things to explore and too many things that simply become distractions.

As she gets older, she will know that objects continue to exist even when they are out of sight. She will manipulate them to see what they can do. As she starts to crawl, encourage her explorations, indoors and outside, through what is real and what is imaginative via books.

Toddler: Continue letting her explore and manipulate objects, giving her your attention and words to name all she is experiencing. Household items can be as interesting, or more so, than store-bought toys. From manipulating and exploring she will move to testing what she can do with something and how it works.

Preschool: Your child has learned about the world of "pretend." It is, however, mixed up with her understanding of reality. Intelligence continues to flourish when she has a wide variety of experiences, the words to tell you about those experiences, and the loving relationships that provide trust and balance. Overstimulation, in which she is presented with more than she can absorb or become involved with, is just as detrimental to the development of intelligence as having too few interesting activities and materials to explore. Most children, no matter how intelligent, are not developmentally ready to learn formal reading skills at preschool age.

School age: She is open to new ideas and information. Now she can learn through verbal means (books) as well as the manipulation of objects and interaction with people. You continue to be important in guiding her increasing knowledge and understanding.

Teenage: The intelligent teenager is now able to manipulate ideas abstractly. She can see all kinds of relationships between ideas that she could not earlier. Do not underestimate her need for guidance, however, particularly if she is very intelligent, in thinking through the implications of what she is learning and exploring.

Influences on learning the value

Needs: Her curiosity, her innate drive to understand, provides the motivation for her to develop her intelligence.

Temperament: Some temperament patterns increase a child's opportunities to learn. One who is very aware of her environment will have access to more information than one who is less aware. One who is persistent is apt to stay with a problem longer, thus learning more about her world and how it works than one who gives up easily.

Learning style: A child with a strong preference may be cut off from sources of information, thus decreasing the extent of her knowledge. Some learning styles increase flexibility of learning and may, therefore, increase the complexity of her thinking. Many brilliant people have poor hand-eye coordination, making hand writing a tedious process. Children with this problem should have access to computers.

Reflections about the value

Influence of other values: Values (first yours, then hers) guide the intelligent child's thinking. Intelligence by itself does not guarantee that a child will make wise decisions, act with consideration towards others, or know how to keep a job. Her intelligence can get in the way of having a fulfilling life if she does not have a strong value system guiding her intelligence.

New thinking resulting from analysis: Separating the value "intelligence" from wisdom and caring shows more clearly the importance of your role as a parent, a guide, to your intelligent child.

Analyzing a Value

Makes thoughtful decisions

Thinking about the value

Definition: Makes careful, considerate choices

Behavior reflecting value: Makes a schedule for doing her homework based on how much she has, how hard it is, and when she is most alert. Decides whether or not she can afford to buy something based on funds available and other plans that require money.

Knowledge and skills needed: She can describe a situation accurately and knows what other information might be relevant and how to find it. She can brainstorm several options. She can recognize that goals, circumstances, and other considerations may have an impact on her decision, and she can analyze her options based on these.

Insights about the value: Making thoughtful decisions is a process that involves knowing what the situation is, being aware of what the choices are, and having guides to help with making the decision. Development of the ability to make thoughtful decisions will be closely linked to a child's mental development.

Value present at birth?___Yes _X_No

Teaching or preserving the value

Baby: Accept baby's signal that she is full. Recognize her ways of telling you she is tired or wet.

Toddler: Encourage her to make simple decisions, such as to have one apple slice or two. Show her the items as that will help her to choose. Teach her the words to describe choices.

Preschool: Help her describe a situation. Encourage her to think of two or three alternatives. Help her make choices in regard to social situations. Point out that it is more fun to play with another person than to play alone.

School age: Help her gather information about a situation. This may mean a trip to the library or exploring the Internet. Encourage her to think of several options. Have her make decisions, accepting the fact that they will be based on absolutes. At this stage of development, something is either right or wrong; there are no gray areas.

Teenage: Allow and encourage her to describe a situation with accuracy, think of many options, accumulate a fund of information on which to base a decision, analyze situations and options, and make a choice based on the information she has.

Influences on learning the value

Needs: Her curiosity is a strong motivator for the development of this ability.

Temperament: If she is an impulsive child who is frequently highly distractible and persistent, it will be hard for her to stop and anticipate consequences of action. However, learning to make thoughtful decisions may help her become less impulsive.

Learning style: If her preferred learning style is visual, for instance, she will find problem solving easier if visual clues, such as lists, pictures, and graphs, are provided and she is shown how to do something.

Reflections about the value

Influence of other values: Being aware is a value that impacts making thoughtful decisions. The more aware a child is of her environment, the people in it and what they are doing, saying, and feeling, the objects in the environment, and what is happening, the more information she will have on which to base her decisions.

New thinking resulting from analysis: It is amazing at what a young age children can start to learn to make decisions. They can think of choices, choose certain ones, and see the results of their choices in their play as early as two years old. Making thoughtful decisions is a process, not an instant event, and parents need to be patient with the learning.

Analyzing a Value

RESPONSIBLE

~~~~~~~~

Thinking about the value

Definition: To assume accountability for something being done or not; to be accountable for an event

Behavior reflecting value: As he becomes a responsible member of society he is able to take care of his basic needs and enter into the life of the community. As he grows up, he will learn to complete his homework on time, get to school on time, and clean up his room, among other responsibilities.

Knowledge and skills needed: To be able to be responsible requires the desire to be so, knowledge of what is expected, and ability to meet those expectations. For example, for him to be responsible for his clothes means he needs to know what is appropriate to wear when, how to put his clothes on, what clothes he needs, how to shop for them, and how to take care of them (washing, dry cleaning, mending). Whatever the responsibility, much knowledge and many skills are needed.

Insights about the value: First, identify what you want him to be responsible for. Then analyze what knowledge and skills he needs to be responsible for that area. It is quite unfair to expect a child to be responsible for getting himself ready to go somewhere, for example, if he does not know how to put his shoes on the right feet, button his clothes, or comb his hair.

Value present at birth?___Yes __X_No

Teaching or preserving the value

Note: List the areas you want him to be responsible for in adulthood. Then analyze each of those areas to see what knowledge and skills he will need to fulfill your expectations. For each area of responsibility, decide at what age you expect him to acquire which information and skills. Clearly, some areas of responsibility require more learning and skills, and therefore time, than others.

The acquiring of knowledge and skills in regard to clothes and dressing at different stages outlined below is based on a responsibility one can assume of a child in adulthood, namely, the ability to dress himself and to choose and care for his clothes. Following the analysis of this value is an analysis of what teenagers need to know to be safe, independent drivers.

Baby: A baby's first responsibility is to learn when he is cold or hot and protest his discomfort. At around four to six months, he will begin to help by putting his arms into sleeves or legs into pants. Reinforce this skill by thanking him and telling him in words what he has just done.

Toddler: A toddler can choose which pants to wear, the blue or the yellow (the dress pants are not offered). He can indicate if he is hot or cold and therefore needs more or less clothing. He can continue to help more with dressing himself and is usually quite capable of undressing himself.

Preschooler: He can choose his clothes. Talk about appropriate clothes for specific occasions. He can dress himself except for the difficult parts, such as getting shoes on the right feet and tying them. He can learn how to get jackets, mittens, and hats on.

School age: By this time, he can dress himself and most likely is choosing the clothes he wants to wear with some comment from you. He is able to run the washing machine and wash his own clothes if you want him to. He can shop with you to learn about prices, costs of popular clothes (brands), and about comfort and durability.

Teenage: A teenager should be able to take care of his clothes, decide what is appropriate to wear, and use good judgment in buying clothes.

Influences on learning the value

Needs: The drive to be accepted and/or loved and to have self-esteem may motivate him to be responsible.

Temperament: Children who are easily distracted have trouble following through on tasks. They may become interested in a book while cleaning their room and hours later be found reading while the room is still a mess. Young children who are distractible may dawdle while dressing, causing the whole family to be late getting out of the house.

A child who has a somber (pessimistic) mood can make you feel guilty for setting expectations. You need to be aware of such a reaction and deal with it if you want to stick to the value of responsibility. Remember, too, that he is not "manipulating" you, it is just how he sees life.

Learning style: If he is a visual learner, make charts and pictures to remind him of what he is supposed to do.

Reflections about the value

Influence of other values: For the sake of his healthy self-esteem, be careful to set expectations that are within reach (some stretching is desirable) and structure them so that he can succeed. Be careful not to call him names or apply labels if he fails.

New thinking resulting from analysis: Analyzing responsibility shows that parents need to think long-term, rather than short-term for a child. It is natural to want him to be responsible for things now, such as toys, clothes, and general mess. However, there are so many skills to learn in order to be able to be responsible. He will learn some skills by watching what you do at home; you will have to teach him other skills quite deliberately.

RESPONSIBLE CAR USE FOR INDEPENDENT DRIVING

(Reprinted with permission from Elizabeth Crary, © 1998)

Legal requirements
• Obtain a learner's permit, and then a driver's license.
• Have car insurance.

Knowledge
• Understand and apply all rules of the road.
• Be able to drive to a new place using a map; be able to locate himself on map and then drive to new place.
• Create a plan to handle emergencies (flat tire, out of gas, dead battery, accident).
• Know how to use emergency items stored in car (car jack, battery cables, flares).

• Know what to do in case of accident (stay at the scene; provide evidence of license and car insurance; get names, addresses, and phone numbers of witnesses; refrain from discussing accident with anyone except police officer; get word to parents).

Skills

Demonstrate ability to drive in these conditions (5 to 20 hours of practice):

night   snow   rain   fog   city
mountain   freeway   rush hour   2-lane road

Demonstrate auto maintenance skills:
• Fill gas tank.
• Change flat tire.
• Check oil, transmission, power steering, brake, water, windshield cleaning fluid levels.
• Check tire pressure.
• Read and understand gauges on car dash.
• Be aware of changes in sound or feel of car that can indicate a problem brewing.

Responsibilities

• Discuss appropriate and inappropriate driving behavior.
• Schedule car use with family.
• Have agreement with parents about giving rides to other people.
• Decide how repairs are paid for if teenager is at fault.
• Decide what share teenager takes for cost of insurance, gas, and oil, if any.
• Determine under what conditions driving privileges are revoked.
• Schedule intervals to review and update driving agreement with parents.

Understanding the big picture

• Know the extra cost to add a teenager (especially a male under age 25) to a car insurance policy.
• Figure out the average cost of repairs per month and per mile driven.
• Figure out the average cost of gas and oil per month and per mile driven.
• Determine costs of ownership, registration, licensing, emissions inspections for one year.

Analyzing a Value

SELF-ESTEEM

Thinking about the value

Definition: Feeling good about oneself; holding oneself in high regard

Behavior reflecting value: She volunteers to answer questions whether she is completely sure of the answer or not. She would assume she was the life of the party if that were her desire. She approaches tasks with the certainty that she can succeed.

Knowledge and skills needed: Self-esteem is a feeling, an attitude toward herself that she either has or does not have.

Insights about the value: Knowing some particular fact or having some particular skill is not the essence of self-esteem. Self-esteem is not taught. It grows as a child experiences that she is valued as a person.

Value present at birth?___Yes _X_ No

Teaching or preserving the value

Baby: By treasuring her, you start to build the foundation for good self-esteem. By satisfying her needs, you build within her a deep sense that she is of value. She learns that if she cries, you will meet her need, that she is worthy of having her need satisfied. She may also be gaining a sense of competency, that is, she can do something (cry) that gets her need met. She recognizes that the world is trustworthy, that she can trust that her needs will be met, and that she herself is worthy. This stage in life is important for laying such a foundation.

Toddler: Your willingness to help her explore her world safely, to help her understand how the world works, and to talk with her about her experiences continues to give her the message that she is a person of worth, building her self-esteem. You are also building her sense of competency, an integral part of self-esteem.

Preschool: The challenge now is to resolve the dilemma of setting expectations for her versus maintaining her good feelings about herself. At this stage she will begin to resist doing some of the things she was so eager to do before (zipping her coat, washing her hands, taking her dishes to the kitchen). Such tasks are no longer challenges, but routines.

One way to handle this dilemma is to take care to watch your language and that of other people around her. Beware of labels that children assume are descriptively accurate. If you call a child who is reluctant to do what you want her to "lazy," "dumb," "stupid," or any number of other labels, you run the risk of her deciding that is who she is. Such negative labels are damaging to self-esteem. Instead, label her behavior: "You seem to be feeling lazy today."

School age: The expectations set by the school can be a real threat to her self-esteem. Children who have any kind of learning disability or simply a different pace in development than the majority of the other children can come to feel they are worthless. Your support and advocacy for her can be a real protection to her feelings of self-worth during these years. Bright children as well as all other children need and deserve such support.

Peers can undermine her self-esteem in many ways. Our culture is full of put-downs (television being one of the most blatant sources in this regard). Helping her to hear the put-downs, analyze them, and speak up against them will give her some protection against this threat.

Teenage: The challenges of elementary school continue into the teen years. She may be less willing to articulate the problems, but they exist. Keep lines of positive communication open, and support and protect her.

Influences on learning the value

Needs: Self-esteem is a basic need. The need to feel good about oneself can motivate her to many kinds of behavior. One of the challenges of parenthood is to help her feel good about herself through behaviors that are healthy rather than destructive.

Temperament: If she is very sensitive emotionally, she will be more vulnerable to any hint that she is less than worthy than will a less sensitive child, who may be stronger in the face of criticism. A child who is very sensitive emotionally, responds intensely, and tends to withdraw will be very challenging as you try to maintain and build her self-esteem.

Learning style: A learning style or disability that makes it difficult for her to learn in school can be devastating to her self-esteem, particularly if she has trouble learning to read, the basis of almost all schoolwork. Whatever the problem, support her through all difficulties.

Reflections about the value

Influence of other values: High expectations for her to be thoughtful and reflective in all matters, to be competent in many areas, to be caring of others at all times can be a threat to her good feelings about herself because it will not be easy for her to meet such expectations. Balance between expectations and acceptance of ability, performance, and self is necessary if she is to have high self-esteem.

New thinking resulting from analysis: Are children born feeling good about themselves?

How can you keep a child feeling good about herself and still hold her to expectations that may be somewhat beyond her present capabilities? Would setting expectations undermine her sense of self-esteem? Or does she feel good about herself because she is growing in capability and competence by trying to meet expectations? Is it good for her to feel good about herself and not be competent, not be able to do things or know things or care about others? How do you find the balance?

To resolve this dilemma, maybe we have to distinguish two separate feelings in a child: one is an inner core of trust that the baby develops by having her needs met routinely; the other is self-esteem. The first gives her a deep sense of self-worth. She acquires the second, self-esteem, as she becomes aware of herself as a person and is able to judge her abilities. Self-esteem is tied to her sense of competence. A child who has high self-esteem (thinks highly of herself) but has no competency in basic skills, such as being able to make good decisions, is headed for trouble. For self-esteem to be more than the emperor's new clothes it must be based on being competent in some areas. Therefore, you must set expectations so that she has something to strive for and something real to feel good about.

Trusting oneself, in contrast, is a premise of self-esteem. Such trust gives a child the faith that she can learn to cope, to make good judgments, and to tell the difference between what she can do well and what she cannot. That trust develops during infancy.

Analyzing a Value

SPIRITUAL

Thinking about the value

Definition: Being aware of the essence of life and the wonder and beauty of the world. Searching for meaning; living life as a sacred journey; being centered

Behavior reflecting value: He responds to beauty; is aware of the mystery of life. He is careful of the environment; picks up trash. He looks for the meaning in what a child says. He notices the similarities as well as the differences in the world's religions, political thought, and philosophies.

Knowledge and skills needed: The ability to meditate helps even a young person stay in touch with and connected to his inner life. Knowledge of the religious stories and beliefs of his parents' faith often gives expression to the spiritual, especially for young children.

Insights about the value: This value is not so much taught as it is lived. Time is of utmost importance: time to be in touch, to envision the relationships and connectedness of the universe. It is also important to have beauty around.

Value present at birth?_X_Yes ___No   It can be seen in the open-eyed stare of the new baby seeing the world of color for the first time. It can be detected in the unborn baby's response in utero to music.

Teaching or preserving the value

Baby/Toddler: Provide beauty in art and music forms. Give him time to enjoy and to wonder. A young child responds to beauty so easily; all you need to do is give him opportunities and time to enjoy it. Include religious stories in what you read to him. Teach him expressions of gratitude, such as prayers or silence before and/or after meals and at bedtime.

Preschool: Continue as before. Help him to respect his environment. For example, teach him not to tear leaves off trees or bash flowers or step on bugs because they too are living beings. Continue to read the stories of your faith to him.

School age/Teenage: Respect his search for meaning. Consider what his music means to him. Guide him to be respectful of the environment and people. Take time to listen to his questions, to be aware of the issues, and to answer his questions honestly.

Influences on learning the value

Needs: Spirituality is a value that is also a basic need, one that often goes unmet in later life for many people. It is easily observable in children's response to beauty.

Temperament: His temperament will influence how he experiences beauty or comes in touch with the essence. An active child may dance to the music while a quiet child sits and listens, both will be moved.

Learning style: Make available to him the experiences to which he is most responsive. They might be music, art, dance, literature, mountain climbing . . . observe him carefully to see what moves him.

Reflections about the value

Influence of other values: Many values, such as caring, being aware, and being cooperative, help children experience connectedness and consequently increase their potential for being spiritual.

New thinking resulting from analysis: It is difficult to say what spiritual means exactly . . . and yet it exists. Perhaps that is one of the reasons people have found so many different expressions for the spiritual aspect of their lives. Thinking about a child's spirituality can strengthen your desire to be aware of his spiritual journey, though it takes a different form from your own or anyone else's.

Family Guide to Parenting with Values in Mind

Identifying My Values

Make a list of the values you wish to see in your child
10 to 30 years from now.

_____	_____
_____	_____
_____	_____
_____	_____
_____	_____
_____	_____

Identifying My Parenting Partner's Values

Make a list of the values your parenting partner (anyone who shares
parenting responsibilities with you) wants to see in the
same child 10 to 30 years from now.

_____	_____
_____	_____
_____	_____
_____	_____
_____	_____
_____	_____

Analyzing a Value

Write your value here _____

Make as many copies of pages 166-167 as you need to analyze each of your values separately.

The numbers in parentheses indicate the chapter where relevant information can be found.

Thinking about the value

Definition (2):

Behavior reflecting value (2):

Knowledge and skills needed (3):

Insights about the value:

Value present at birth (3)?____Yes ____No

Teaching or preserving the value

Baby (6):

Toddler (6):

Preschool (6):

School age (6):

Teenage (6):

Influences on learning the value
Needs (5):

Temperament (7):

Learning style (8):

Reflections about the value
Influence of other values (9):

New thinking resulting from analysis:

Resolving My Conflicting Values

This exercise will help you identify and deal with conflicts between your personal values.

Relationships between values

List values that support each other.

List your values that help other values to develop.

Value	Other value	Help in this way

List and describe pairs of values in conflict.

Examples of kinds of possible conflict are:

• One value teaches undesirable behavior according to the other value.

• One value sets expectations that conflict with the other value.

• Acting on one value lessens the likelihood of child gaining skills relevant to the other value.

Pair of values	Conflict	Impact on parenting

How is each value important?

"Being_____is important to me
because:_____."

There are many reasons; some possible ones are:

• Value is based on a moral principle.

• The world would be a better place if everyone lived by this value.

• Living by this value leads to self-fulfillment.

• Value is based on expectations set by the society I live in, or by gender roles, civic responsibilities, family standards, etc.

Describe what the world would be like if all people held this value.

When and why might you consider not honoring this value?

Resolving conflict between values

What ways do you see to resolve the conflict?

Example: A value based on a social stereotype seems less important now and does not need to be honored.

Can consideration of development resolve the conflict?

Example: Allowing a very young child to be curious about everything, as is her nature, and expecting her to satisfy her curiosity without touching when she is older (being respectful of others' property).

What basic needs, if any, do the conflicting values address?

Example: Child is very hungry and all that is available is soda pop and glazed donuts (food vs. health).

What different way of behaving could resolve the conflict?

Example: Asking a child to keep her opinions to herself around strangers, but allowing her to say whatever is on her mind in private.

What similar aspects among the values might lead to resolution?

Example: Helping a child develop good judgment would allow her to be both caring and competitive.

Resolving Conflicting Values Between My Partner and Me

This exercise will help you and your parenting partner (anyone who shares parenting responsibilities with you) deal with conflicts between the values you each hold.

Relationships between your values and your partner's

List values you have in common.

List supporting values.

List your values that help other values to develop.

Value   *Other value*   *Help in this way*

List and describe pairs of values in conflict.
Examples of kinds of possible conflict are:
• One value teaches undesirable behavior according to the other value.
• One value sets expectations that conflict with the other value.
• Acting on one value lessens the likelihood of child gaining skills relevant to the other value.

Pair of values   *Conflict*   *Impact on parenting*

How is each value important?
"Being_____is important to me because:_____."

There are many reasons; some possible ones are:
• Value is based on a moral principle.
• The world would be a better place if everyone lived by this value.

• Living by this value leads to self-fulfillment.
• Value is based on expectations set by the society I live in, or by gender roles, civic responsibilities, family standards, etc.

Describe what the world would be like if all people held this value.

When and why might you consider not honoring this value?

Resolving conflict between values

What ways do you see to resolve the conflict?
Example: Recognizing that sometimes it is not appropriate to honor one value over another, as children playing sports know they are to be competitive in that situation, not caring of the other teams' feelings.

Can consideration of development resolve the conflict?
Example: Understanding that a young child who is very tired and unruly needs a nap, not further pressure to be quiet, still, and polite.

What basic needs, if any, do the conflicting values address?
Example: Preschooler wants to help wash dishes (safety vs. competency).

What different way of behaving could resolve the conflict?
Example: Allowing child to have one area of the house in which he confines the mess of creativity.

What similar aspects among the values might lead to resolution?
Example: Developing a child's intelligence would allow him to learn many different ways to satisfy his curiosity.

Helpful Resources

The number of useful books for parents seems unlimited. The books suggested here are specific to the discussion of values. Some, such as those on development, cover a topic important to integrating values into family life in greater detail. Others, like those on teaching problem solving, are exceptional for helping you teach skills relevant to learning values.

No books on discipline or child guidance are included because there are many good ones. You will need to find the methods best suited to your parenting style, your children, and your family. You might browse the shelves of your favorite bookstore or the Internet for possibilities.

BOOKS ON DEVELOPMENT

Dan Riley School for a Girl: An Adventure in Home Schooling, The by Dan Riley. New York: Houghton Mifflin Co., 1994. This book describes so beautifully the growing relationship between a dad and his daughter. It also gives illustrations of how he managed to change their relationship dramatically.

First Feelings: Milestones in the Emotional Development of Your Baby and Child by Stanley Greenspan and Nancy Greenspan. New York: Viking Press, 1985. This is a good description of infant development. The author's approach (emotions) provides a balance to the development of thinking discussed in *Using Your Values. . . .*

How to Live Almost Happily with a Teenager by Lois Davitz and Joel Davitz. Minneapolis: Winston Press, Inc., 1982. This excellent book gives a useful description of adolescence as a developmental stage. Look for it in your public library.

Playground Politics: Understanding the Emotional Life of Your School-age Child by Stanley Greenspan and Jacqueline Salmon. Reading, Mass.: Addison Wesley, 1993. This book describes children's development in the school-age years.

BOOKS ON FEELINGS

All My Feelings at Home: Ellie's Day by Susan Friedman and Susan Conlin. Seattle: Parenting Press, Inc., 1989.

Dealing with Feelings series: I'm Excited; I'm Frustrated; I'm Furious; I'm Mad; I'm Proud; I'm Scared by Elizabeth Crary. Seattle: Parenting Press, Inc., 1992 and 1994.

What Is A Feeling? by David Krueger, M.D. Seattle: Parenting Press, Inc., 1993.

BOOKS ON PROBLEM SOLVING

Children's Problem Solving series: I Can't Wait; I Want It; I Want to Play; I'm Lost; Mommy, Don't Go; My Name Is Not Dummy, Second edition, by Elizabeth Crary. Seattle: Parenting Press, Inc., 1996.

Raising a Thinking Child: Help Your Young Child to Resolve Everyday Conflicts and Get Along with Others by Myrna Shure. New York: Henry Holt and Co., 1994.

BOOK ON TEMPERAMENT

Understanding Temperament: Strategies for Creating Family Harmony by Lyndall Shick, M.A. Seattle: Parenting Press, Inc., 1998.

USEFUL WEB SITES

Information on temperament: *http://www.preventiveoz.org*

Information on values and the research demonstrating the importance of values in the lives of people: *http://www.conrowpub.com*

"Parenting Tip of the Week" and information on all Parenting Press publications for parents and parenting education practitioners: *http://www. parentingpress.com*

Index

Practical Books for Thoughtful Parents

Time-In: When Time-Out Doesn't Work by Jean Illsley Clarke. With the use of four tools, **Ask, Act, Attend,** and **Amend,** the author shows parents how to establish strong connections with their children. Useful with birth to 10 years. 82 pages. $9.95 paperback

Pick Up Your Socks . . . and Other Skills Growing Children Need! by Elizabeth Crary. Parents can teach responsibility. Includes research on when children typically handle household chores. Useful with ages 3-15 years. 112 pages. $14.95 paperback

Grounded for Life?! Stop Blowing Your Fuse and Start Communicating with Your Teenager by Louise Felton Tracy, M.A. School counselor and mother of six shows parents how to turn unproductive, unpleasant years with teens into growth-filled, satisfying years. Useful with 10-18 years. 164 pages. $12.95 paperback. **Parents' Choice award.**

Understanding Temperament: Strategies for Creating Family Harmony by Lyndall Shick, M.A. When parents know why family members behave as they do, and how to manage their behavior, they can change family conflict into cooperation. Useful with all ages. 126 pages. $13.95 paperback

PARENTING PRESS, INC.
Dept. 201, P.O. Box 75267 / Seattle, Washington 98125
Toll free 1-800-992-6657

In Canada, call Raincoast Books Distribution Co.,
1-800-663-5714
Prices subject to change without notice